Structured Spreadsheet Modelling and Implementation

A Methodology for Creating Effective Spreadsheets

Second Edition

By Paul Mireault

SSMI International

Structured Spreadsheet Modelling and Implementation

by Paul Mireault

Second Edition

ISBN 978-0-9948834-3-8

SSMI International Inc.

URL: www.ssmi.international

Email: book@ssmi.international

Table of Contents

Table of Tables

Table of Figures

Preface to the Second Edition

The main reason for producing this second edition comes from feedback I received from spreadsheet developers as well as academics to whom I presented the SSMI methodology.

I did a lot of computer programming during some periods in my studies and my career, and the term *parameter* has a very specific meaning to me: it is a value supplied to a program (or a function, or a module) so it can perform some calculation and produce a result. So, it was natural for me to use that term to refer to the constants that are used in a spreadsheet. When talking to people who did not have a programming background, like most spreadsheet developers working in different business activities like finance and accounting, and like many academics teaching in similar areas, I almost always got the reaction "Oh! You mean *data*."

Since I developed SSMI for the spreadsheet developers, not for programmers, there was no reason for me to use a term that did not convey the proper meaning. So, I did a major nomenclature change: *parameter* became *data* throughout the book.

I also took the occasion to correct errors in the text and in some figures.

Foreword

In my 35-year teaching experience, I've always striven to make sure that my students learn the best strategies for creating effective, error-free spreadsheets. What interests me most, after my decades of teaching, is the way spreadsheet literacy is taught—or, often, not taught.

I've never liked the way Excel is typically taught in business schools, where lectures are either template-based or "point-and-click"-oriented. In these types of courses, students rarely understand how to conceptualize a problem and translate it into a spreadsheet, from start to finish. So, I developed a methodology that would teach students exactly that: how to *use* Excel.

(Of course, Excel isn't the only spreadsheet software available today. But since it's arguably the most widely available tool, and the one students are most likely to be familiar with, in this book I focus on that particular program.)

Whenever I address audiences—whether they're undergraduates, MBAs or executives—I always ask them: "How did you learn to use Excel?" Most people say they "learned by doing"— sometimes with the help of colleagues, who would show them a few tricks. Only a few actually attended classes, and these were generally short (from a few hours to a couple of days).

Such brief exposure doesn't make a person very adept at using this tool. Those classes generally show only what Excel can do—the different functions available—rather than what people really need to know: how to use the software in a business context.

This approach gives no real instruction on modelling, to contextualize how the tool is used—an aspect that's often neglected. As a result, the experience is like trying to learn a language by reading a dictionary. You may learn the meaning of the words (the what), but not the syntax, structure or subtleties (the how).

The same can be said of books. They may explain all Excel's features, menus and functions; they may even describe how to use the program in specific contexts such as finance, accounting, or marketing. But they do not always offer the business cases that users need.

Another drawback is that they generally present students with a "blank canvas," or at best only a limited number of templates—and leave it to readers to figure out how to modify or adapt them to their specific needs.

My book, however, takes a different approach. Instead of showing readers many examples to teach them how to develop spreadsheets, it presents a methodology that they can apply to a wide range of situations and needs.

Excel itself follows precise rules, specifically designed to reduce the possibility of errors—both during the initial creation of a spreadsheet, and during its later maintenance or modification. My methodology builds on this foundation to make the process easier and less error-prone.

In my view, two of the major problems that bedevil new Excel users are the illusions of simplicity and productivity—as I describe below.

The Illusion of Simplicity. One of the reasons Excel is such a powerful and popular tool is its relative lack of structure. This "free-form" concept often appeals to novice users, who are comforted by its lack of intimidating detail. But as they become more experienced with the program, they often impose some structure of their own. They may identify input cells with colour, format the labels that describe the cells' content, or separate data from formulas in different areas of their spreadsheets.

In my view, this apparent need for self-imposed structure indicates that the simplicity of Excel is an illusion. More to the point, this lack of structure hinders the program's ability to be shared, maintained and audited.

Let me illustrate this with an analogy. Many industries have adopted codes—rules that guide people on what the accepted norms are. All kind of professionals—plumbers and engineers, dentists and architects, drivers and chefs—are taught the importance of norms, and must follow strict guidelines.

Electricians, for example, must use certain colours to differentiate specific types of wires. Nobody disputes the benefit of this: all-black wiring would be problematic, even dangerous. The different colours signal to all electricians exactly what has been done, allowing one person to work on wiring installed by someone else—even many years later.

The same is true for software programmers, who also often use coding conventions for tasks such as naming variables. As with electricians, this allows one programmer—perhaps the person responsible for maintenance—to see at a glance what the original programmer did, and what previous modifications may have been made. Otherwise, they would have to spend hours trying to understand the original intent.

This is a major benefit of such standards: they allow work to be handed off. This concept—passing on a spreadsheet to someone else, either for their personal use or for further development—is one of the major benefits of the SSMI approach.

I'd like to emphasize this point, simply because—under existing conditions—the handing off of a spreadsheet from one person to another is often simply not possible. Most users have no training in using norms, and are usually on their own when defining the terms they need.

And because any spreadsheet they create is based on nothing more than their personal preferences, it can't easily be interpreted by others who are unfamiliar with the norms they invented and used. (It may even become a mystery to the creator, who a few weeks later may have forgotten the original principles!)

That fact leads to the second common illusion.

The Illusion of Productivity. Most people fire up Excel in order to solve a specific problem—and then they sit and stare at Cell A1, thinking: "What do I do now?!" They may start by writing a few labels and formulas. They decide that these don't do the job; they delete their work; look up some Help topics; go in another direction; try another approach; find it's a dead end; and so on.

In fact, a study of the typical spreadsheet creation process found that most participants spent very little time planning their strategy before launching into the creation process; and they then spent 21% of their time pausing—presumably to engage in the above activities[1].

Eventually these people either achieve some kind of result, or give up in frustration. But either way, this is a futile and time-wasting process. Such users are under the impression that they're being productive, but that's an illusion.

So what can be done to disillusion Excel users? I like to think that the best strategy is to learn to use the SSMI methodology, which I introduce in this book. Quite simply, its goal is to make it simpler for you to become more productive at creating effective spreadsheets.

---

[1] Brown, P. S., & Gould, J. D. (1987). An Experimental Study of People Creating Spreadsheets. ACM Transactions on Office Information Systems. "Participants spent 21 percent of their time pausing, presumably reading and/or thinking, prior to the initial keystrokes of spreadsheet creation episodes."

I developed the process from proven concepts used in the fields of information systems and software engineering, and fine-tuned it over twenty years of teaching. The aim of this methodology is to reorient users to splitting the creative process in two: first developing a model, and then implementing the model as a spreadsheet. This book teaches you to treat those activities as separate, with the one a necessary precursor to the other.

What exactly does **Structured Spreadsheet Modelling and Implementation** mean?

Structured Spreadsheet. As I mentioned above, Excel's relative lack of structure hinders many users from using the program as well as they might. It limits the extensibility of a spreadsheet, and its ability to be shared. SSMI methodology focuses on teaching developers how to structure their spreadsheets. A well-constructed spreadsheet should be quick and easy for people to understand—so it can be easily handed off to other developers, or understood by colleagues, bosses, clients, auditors, etc.

Modelling. The basis of the SSMI methodology is the separation of creative and mechanical tasks. The activity of spreadsheet modelling—the creative process—is how you conceptualize the problem. The idea is to build the model without even touching Excel. This allows you to focus on the conceptual process, and relieves you of the need to refer to the software.

Implementation. This is the industry term for translating the conceptual model of the problem into a spreadsheet. Since effective implementation depends almost totally on effective modelling, the SSMI methodology renders this mechanical process relatively straightforward.

Using this methodology has many benefits—both for users (the people whose work depends on the spreadsheets), and even more for developers (the people who create the spreadsheets). When developers follow SSMI methods, both they and the users find it faster and easier to:

- understand what they're doing when they create a spreadsheet, which reduces the probability of errors;
- review a spreadsheet, and test it for errors;
- explain to others how a spreadsheet works;
- modify a spreadsheet to adapt it to changing situations;
- maintain a spreadsheet throughout its lifecycle;
- manage a spreadsheet in an organizational setting.

To cover all this material, and to show you in detail how to become a spreadsheet expert, this book is divided into three parts.

Part I provides a general overview of the spreadsheet development process (Chapter 1).

Part II introduces a case study: Marco's Widgets, a fictional company I'll use throughout much of the book to illustrate SSMI principles and processes. Part II also explains the three main types of spreadsheet model, and outlines how to apply the methodology—including how to:

- understand basic SSMI concepts (Chapter 2)
- develop a simple model (Chapter 3)
- implement a simple model (Chapter 4)
- develop a repeating sub-model (Chapter 5)
- implement a repeating sub-model (Chapter 6)
- understand time in a spreadsheet (Chapter 7)
- develop a temporal model (Chapter 8)
- implement a temporal model (Chapter 9).

Part III looks at more advanced spreadsheet techniques, including how to:

- modify a model (Chapter 10)
- learn modelling techniques (Chapter 11)
- manage spreadsheets (Chapter 12).

Finally, the book concludes with Appendices that give extra information and reference material.

Part I: Introducing SSMI

Chapter 1: Understanding Spreadsheets

- Managing Spreadsheet Risk
- Understanding the Spreadsheet Life Cycle
- Developing Information Systems
- Developing a Spreadsheet

Chapter 1   Understanding Spreadsheets

How to use this chapter

This chapter is a leisurely read. Pay attention to the importance of the conceptual model, which is a way of representing your problem without referencing the technology that will be used for the implementation. This is a key concept of the SSMI methodology.

Managing Spreadsheet Risk

For many people nowadays, the spreadsheet is a work tool they can't imagine living without. A powerful and flexible way to accomplish many common tasks, spreadsheets are widely used in a variety of fields. Despite this ubiquity, however, the sad truth is that most spreadsheets—over 90%, according to some research—contain at least one error[2].

And all these errors can lead to serious consequences. Depending on the area the spreadsheet is used in, results might include losses of things such as profits, share value, investor or shareholder confidence, financial reputations, or even loss of jobs or careers. Other damage might include false declarations, public embarrassment, overestimation of revenues, underestimation of costs, extra audit costs, and so on. Spreadsheet errors can cause a whole lineup of horror stories.

Some of the most notorious of these include the following news items.

- An accounting error in a financial reporting spreadsheet that wrongly valued a British pension-fund deficit, leading to a £4.3 million write-down of profits (and the resignation of the company's CEO)[3].
- At the 2012 London Olympic Games, an error in a spreadsheet caused 10,000 more tickets to be sold than there were seats for a synchronized swimming event—leading to a lot of frustrated spectators[4].

---

[2] Panko, R. R. (2015). What We Don't Know About Spreadsheet Errors Today: The Facts, Why We Don't Believe Them, and What We Need to Do. *The European Spreadsheet Risks Interest Group 17th Annual Conference*. London.

[3] Daily Express (2011, October 7). Mouchel Profits Blow.
http://www.express.co.uk/finance/city/276053/Mouchel-profits-blow

[4] Kelso, P. (2012, January 4). London 2012 Olympics: Lucky Few to Get 100m Final Tickets After Synchronized Swimming Was Overbooked by 10,000.

- An error in a decision support spreadsheet caused the loss of $2.4 billion for the financial giant JPMorgan Chase. The company's internal review procedure failed to catch the error, which meant that the difference in rates was divided by their sum, rather than by their average[5].

- An error in a data analysis spreadsheet led some economics researchers to wrong conclusions. Unfortunately, this was discovered only after their research paper was published, and used as a basis for government economic policies[6].

The consequence of such a high error rate is that many executives now distrust the accuracy of spreadsheets, and worry that decision-makers are not getting the full benefit from the time and effort spent building complex models[7]. One result has been an increase in the activity of spreadsheet verification. Some large businesses now have internal groups dedicated to auditing the organization's spreadsheets.

But although this aspect of risk governance and control is important, it's also often an extremely tedious and time-consuming task—and hence is sometimes even skipped altogether. This is especially true when spreadsheets lack consistency. This is why the SSMI methodology insists on building consistent spreadsheets right from the beginning of their life cycle.

Understanding the Spreadsheet Life Cycle

Most spreadsheets start their lives as productivity tools, developed to meet a specific need. To illustrate the real-world usefulness of the SSMI methodology, let's look at a typical such tool.

David works in the marketing department of a kitchen appliance company, where he's responsible for product management. He built a spreadsheet to keep track of the activities in the product lines he supervises. Because he's the only user, and he knows its workings

http://www.telegraph.co.uk/sport/olympics/8992490/London-2012-Olympics-lucky-few-to-get-100m-final-tickets-after-synchronised-swimming-was-overbooked-by-10000.html

[5] Durden, T. (2013, December 2). How a Rookie Excel Error Led JPMorgan to Misreport its VaR for Years. http://www.zerohedge.com/news/2013-02-12/how-rookie-excel-error-led-jpmorgan-misreport-its-var-years

[6] Konczal, M. (2013, April 16). Researchers Finally Replicated Reinhart-Rogoff, and There Are Serious Problems. http://www.nextnewdeal.net/rortybomb/researchers-finally-replicated-reinhart-rogoff-and-there-are-serious-problems

[7] IBM Cognos BI and Performance Management. (2009, January). Spreadsheet-Based Planning: Rough Road Ahead. Information Management.

intimately, he doesn't need any documentation. Any codes or norms are in his own head; any errors affect only him; and any corrections he makes don't need to be passed on to others.

However, his spreadsheet makes David so productive that his colleagues (the other product managers) clue in to the existence of this useful tool, and beg him for a copy. David's a nice guy, willing to share, so he spends some time showing them how to use it. As word spreads, and more people want in on the action, he has to spend more and more of his time training his colleagues and answering their questions. He decides to document his spreadsheet by writing labels that are more descriptive.

Colleagues like his tool so much that they start suggesting modifications and enhancements, to make it more useful to them. David is in a quandary. On the one hand, he derives some satisfaction from being appreciated by his peers. But on the other hand, the task of improving his creation is taking many hours of time away from his own work. Unless he can convince his boss to acknowledge the valuable contribution he is making to the overall organization, his spreadsheet will actually have a negative impact on his own performance.

Let's say that David's spreadsheet does become an accepted business tool, one his colleagues all depend on. But a few years later, he leaves the company. What happens then? People can continue to use his program—but unless another expert can be found to maintain and upgrade it, it will gradually become less and less useful. It may become the kind of tool commonly known to engineers as a black box: a device that people use without actually knowing how it works. David's former co-workers may still plug information into his system, and get results out of it. But unfortunately, nobody knows exactly how the results were obtained.

In fact, such a story is quite common. Research has shown that the lifespan of the average spreadsheet is five years, and in that time it's usually used by twelve different people[8]. Given this fact, it is important to create spreadsheets that can be understood, maintained and modified by any of the people who use it during its lifetime. This means reducing a spreadsheet's opacity. In this situation, for instance, if David had created a structured spreadsheet from the beginning, he would not have had to spend so much time explaining it, and training his coworkers.

---

[8] Hermans, F. (2012). Analyzing and Visualizing Spreadsheets. PhD Thesis, Technische Universiteit Delft.

To address these issues, it helps spreadsheet developers to be familiar with some basic concepts from other fields, such as software engineering and computer science. Particularly important is the field of information systems, which I'll describe below.

Developing Information Systems

I'll begin by briefly showing you how information systems are generally developed—the typical process of analysis, design and implementation.

An information system is the set of tools—computer programs, databases, and processes—that are needed to make an organization function efficiently. Over the years, Information Systems specialists have devised a methodology to help the Information Technology (IT) developers to create systems that satisfy their users' requirements. This methodology ensures that the creators fully understand even complex processes before they begin the actual programming.

In this section, I will describe the three models of the typical development process for information systems:

- the **physical model** is a set of data tables created with an SQL statement, and managed by a database management system;
- the **logical model** is represented by a data structure diagram, a description of data tables that specifies the relationships between them;
- the **conceptual model** is represented with a diagram in Unified Modelling Language.

These three models are illustrated in Figure 1-1. In this simplified view, they are used in succession. Even though the process appears to be sequential, feedback loops allow for changes to previous steps. I explain the three models (in reverse order) in more detail below.

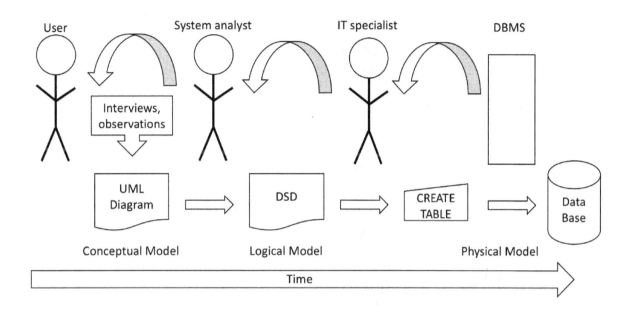

Figure 1-1 Information System Analysis, Design and Implementation

The physical model. An actual implementation of the information system. In a relational database system, this model is managed by a Database Management System (DBMS) such as Oracle, Microsoft SQL Server, or IBM DB2. The two SQL statements in Figure 1-2 serve to create the tables that will contain the data describing each cruise and its stops. They also tell the DBMS how the tables are linked, for example, the table *STOP* is linked to the table *CRUISE* through the column *CRUISECODE*. As shown in Figure 1-2 the set of data tables is created with the SQL statement *CREATE TABLE*.

```
CREATE TABLE CRUISE(
    CRUISECODE     INTEGER NOT NULL,
    CRUISENAME     VARCHAR2(100) NOT NULL,
    SHIPNO         INTEGER NOT NULL,
    DEPARTURE_PORT VARCHAR2(100) NOT NULL,
    ARRIVAL_PORT   VARCHAR2(100) NOT NULL,
    CONSTRAINT CRUISE_PK
        PRIMARY KEY(CRUISECODE),
    CONSTRAINT CRUISE_FK_SHIP
        FOREIGN KEY(SHIPNO) REFERENCES SHIP(SHIPNO));

CREATE TABLE STOP(
    CRUISECODE     INTEGER NOT NULL,
    STOPNO         INTEGER NOT NULL,
    PORT           VARCHAR2(100) NOT NULL,
    ARRIVAL_DAY    INTEGER,
    ARRIVAL_HOUR   INTEGER,
    DEPARTURE_DAY  INTEGER,
    DEPARTURE_HOUR INTEGER,
    CONSTRAINT STOP_PK
        PRIMARY KEY (CRUISECODE,STOPNO),
    CONSTRAINT STOP_FK_CRUISE
        FOREIGN KEY(CRUISECODE) REFERENCES CRUISE(CRUISECODE));
```

Figure 1-2 Physical Model, SQL Statements

Because the physical model is very technical, and requires a specialized vocabulary, the task of implementing it falls to the IT specialists. In order to accomplish this, they need the information provided in the logical model.

The logical model. An overview of the structure of the database, often using tables and relationships with all the information IT specialist needs to write the physical model. This can be represented with a Data Structure Diagram (DSD), as shown in Figure 1-3. The DSD, a high-level description of all the data tables and their fields, can be considered a translation of the user's database requirements into terms the IT specialist can use. However, while these concepts are essential for a proper implementation, it's not strictly necessary for most users to understand the language.

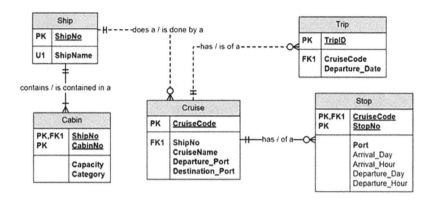

Figure 1-3 Logical Model, DSD of a Cruise Ship

What this database system needs is a way for users to convey their requirements down the chain. This is done with the conceptual model, where the system analyst represents the information in a way that can be understood by the IT specialist.

The conceptual model. A graphical representation of information that the user already knows in a language that can also be understood and manipulated technically by the system analyst—often represented by Unified Modelling Language (UML) diagram. An important characteristic of the conceptual model is that it does not use any technical concepts or depend on a specific technology; instead, it uses ordinary vocabulary—often specific to the user's domain. It translates what the user wants into terms the IT specialists can understand technically. The UML Diagram is usually designed after interviewing users and observing their work processes. Figure 1-4 shows the relationship between different elements of a cruise ship in a conceptual model: it has a specific number of cabins, it stops at specific places, and it sails on specific dates.

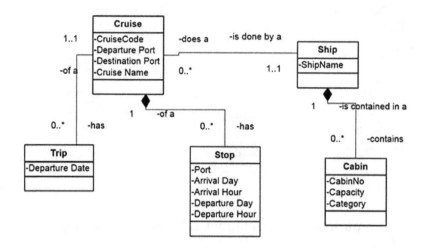

Figure 1-4 Conceptual Model, UML Diagram of Cruise Ship

In information systems, it's common practice to separate the development process into three modelling activities involving the physical, logical, and conceptual models. This means that each party sticks to what they know, and need not waste time (or risk misinterpreting vocabulary) in the other steps of the process.

At present, the area of spreadsheet development is nowhere close to this kind of process optimization. As a result, users are constantly interrupting their creative activity with mechanical tasks, and rarely take the time to reflect on what's necessary to construct a sound model. This book attempts to advise users on how to break down model development in the same kind of steps as information systems.

Developing a Spreadsheet

As mentioned above, most people, when they build spreadsheets, alternate between creative activities (thinking about formulas and variables) and mechanical activities: typing formulas, pointing to cells, copying and testing formulas, etc. As a spreadsheet becomes more complex, these operations take longer to perform; and the more operations there are, the more likely it is that errors will creep in.

One reason for this is that most people—even though they know their own fields well—are not formally trained in information technology; and often creating spreadsheets is only a small part of their job. Figure 1-5 illustrates this "unstructured" design process—a popular one in the world of spreadsheet modelling.

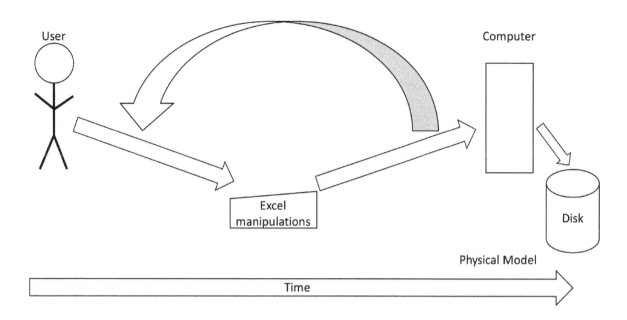

Figure 1-5 Spreadsheet Analysis, Design and Implementation

Now, let's look back at those process models introduced in the last section, Developing Information Systems, and apply them to the spreadsheet development process.

- The **Conceptual Model**: In spreadsheet development, the very heart of this model is the ***Formula Diagram***, described in detail below. This is a graphical representation, designed to provide a quick visual overview of the relationships between variables.

- The **Logical Model**: Created at the same time as the Formula Diagram, this model consists of a ***Formula List*** that describes each variable. Data variables are defined with initial values, and calculated variables by formulas.

- The **Physical Model**: This is the activity that is designed to produce the actual spreadsheet. This process consists merely of mechanical manipulations, and requires no conceptual thought. Although some organizations have developed their own standards for domain-specific spreadsheet applications, these tend to focus on the physical model—with little or no mention of the conceptual and logical models.

Figure 1-6 illustrates these three structured models in the Spreadsheet Design Process.

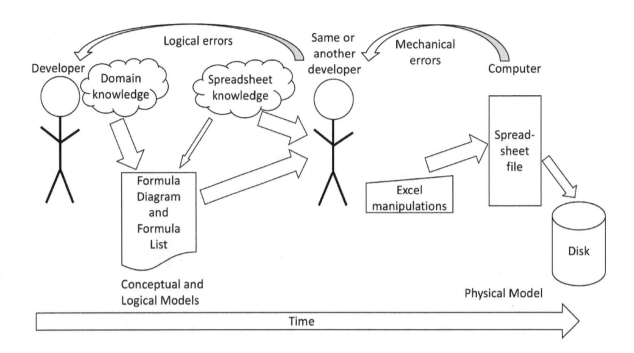

Figure 1-6 SSMI Process

In making this distinction between the creative and mechanical tasks, as it's done in information systems, the spreadsheet development process becomes much more transparent. With the conceptual and logical models, the creation of the physical model is extremely straightforward—it can even be handed off to a different developer.

Professionals never start writing computer programs without first using many different analysis tools (such as flowcharts and data diagrams) to create a clear picture of the program's purpose. After this planning, by the time they begin to actually develop the program, the process is straightforward and requires less exertion of creativity.

Spreadsheet development benefits from a similar approach, separating the two tasks of modelling (the conceptual and logical tasks) and implementation (the physical task of actually creating the spreadsheet). This perception is the heart of the SSMI methodology, which distinguishes between the activities of spreadsheet modelling—the creative process—and spreadsheet design—the mechanical process.

To be most effective, these two tasks must be done separately. That said, the value of each is entirely dependent on the other. Successful implementation depends on a well-structured model; but even the best-structured model is useless if its implementation is haphazard.

Part I Overview

Here are the main points for you to remember from Chapter 1 and Part I.

- Most spreadsheets (about 90%) contain errors. As a developer, you should be aware of this risk, and not be over-confident in your creation.

- The best way to mitigate this risk is by creating properly documented and structured spreadsheets from the start.

- As a developer, you can learn from the field of information systems—which separates the task of creating a system into three models: the conceptual, the logical and the physical.

- Your best strategy is to apply this concept to spreadsheet development, creating a Formula Diagram (conceptual), a Formula List (logical), and a Spreadsheet (physical).

- This approach separates the creative task from the mechanical operations, preventing interference between the two.

Now that you understand the genesis of SSMI methodology, Chapter 2 presents some practical instruction, including a case study.

Part II: Learning the SSMI Methodology

Chapter 2: Understanding the SSMI Methodology

- Learning the Components of a Structured Model
- Using Modelling Rules
- Case Study: Marco's Widgets

Chapter 3: Developing a Simple Model

Chapter 4: Implementing a Simple Model

- Using Three-Tier Architecture
- Using Cell Names
- Using Modules
- Moving from Formula Diagram to Spreadsheet

Chapter 5: Developing a Repeating Sub-Model

- Modelling Without a Repeating Sub-Model
- Modelling With a Repeating Sub-Model
- Conceptualizing Aggregate Functions

Chapter 6: Implementing a Repeating Sub-Model

- Implementing Aggregate Functions
- Exercise: Expanding Regions

Chapter 7: Understanding Time in a Spreadsheet

- Using the Inventory Formula

Chapter 8: Developing a Temporal Model

- Marco's Widgets With Monthly Demand
- Temporal Formula Diagram

Chapter 9: Implementing a Temporal Model

- Implementing a Three-Tier Architecture
- Implementation Sequence

Chapter 2   Understanding the SSMI Methodology

How to use this chapter

This chapter is a leisurely read. It introduces the components of structured modelling and shows how they are implemented. Everything will be explained in detail in the following chapters. It also presents the simple case study that will be used throughout the book.

Modelling is not an easy task for the developer. It's a creative process that creates links between variables using formulas to compute the values. To do this successfully, you must have a certain facility with math and logic.

You should also be familiar with the principles of the specific field you're working in. For instance, if you're building a model designed to make decisions in the field of business management, it's important to know about the concepts of managing inventory, sales force, human resources, etc.

While input and output variables are usually fairly easy to determine, the calculated variables require some imagination. This is not necessarily the kind of artistic imagination you need to write a book or paint a picture. Rather, it's a more structured way of thinking that can visualize the relationships between variables, and represent them as precise formulas.

Later in this chapter, I'll introduce a case study that will be used as a step-by-step demonstration of the SSMI methodology. My goal is to help you to understand the fundamentals by using a relatively simple business situation, with common problems. I'll explain how to create spreadsheets for these models, which can be used for more efficient decision-making. This process can then be scaled up to deal with larger and more complex models.

Learning the Components of a Structured Model

The modelling process we're about to develop has two major components: a Formula List, and a Formula Diagram.

The Formula List is a definition of all the variables, giving their name, values or mathematical formulas. These variables are categorized into four types:

- **data variables**
- **input variables**

- **calculated variables**
- **output variables**.

An example of a simple Formula List is shown in Table 2-1.

Table 2-1 Example of a Formula List

Variable	Type	Definition
Price	Input	**$375**
Profit	Output	**Total Revenue – Total Cost**
DemParA	Data	**376,000**
DemParB	Data	**1.009**
Demand	Calculated	**DemParA * DemParB^–Price**

The Formula Diagram: a graphic representation of the variables and their relationships. Figure 2-1 (a copy of Figure 3-7, from the next chapter) shows how a simple Formula Diagram looks.

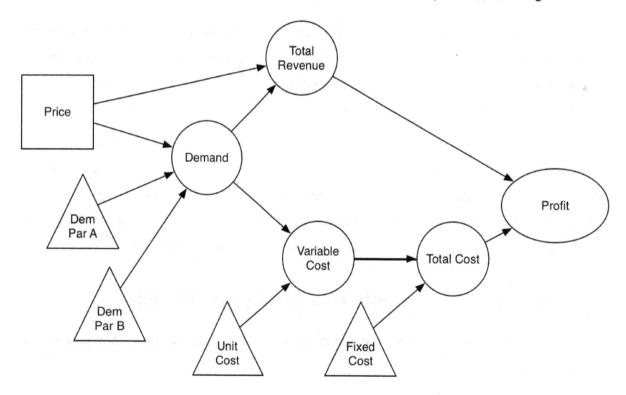

Figure 2-1 Example of a Formula Diagram

I define all these types in more detail below; but first, a note about the formatting you'll see in the following material. To give you a quick visual guide, I've set all the *variable names* and *formulas*—everything you can enter into an Excel cell—in a ***bold and italic*** font. This means when you see something in that kind of type, you know it's a cell entry.

Using Modelling Rules

When a formula contains only a few elements, it's easy to explain and share with others—and also easy to maintain or modify.

Mathematically, the same result is obtained with each of the two alternatives shown in Figure 2-2. But one is more easily comprehensible than the other. In the top left-hand cell are four numbers: $2,500,000, 13,062, $180 and $4,851,160. Looking at this, a reader might need time to understand and validate the underlying formula.

By contrast, the right-hand side of the spreadsheet shows the structured implementation created from the Formula Diagram. Without even having to look at the formula in the cell, each block can be readily understood.

Fixed Cost	$2,500,000		Demand	13,062
Demand	13,062		Unit Cost	$180
Unit Cost	$180		*Variable Cost*	*$2,351,110*
Total Cost	*$4,851,110*			
			Variable Cost	$2,351,110
			Fixed Cost	$2,500,000
			Total Cost	*$4,851,110*

Figure 2-2 Two Modelling Alternatives, Normal View

Fixed Cost	=Fixed_Cost		Demand	=Demand
Demand	=Demand		Unit Cost	=Unit_Cost
Unit Cost	=Unit_Cost		*Variable Cost*	*=E1*E2*
Total Cost	*=B1+B3*B2*			
			Variable Cost	=Variable_Cost
			Fixed Cost	=Fixed_Cost
			Total Cost	*=SUM(E5,E6)*

Figure 2-3 Two Modelling Alternatives, Formula View

It's generally preferable to have more variables with simple formulas, rather than fewer variables with complex formulas. This leads me to state the important Simplicity Rule:

Formulas should not mix different operators.

In other words, users should not mix addition with multiplication, division or functions. They should deconstruct complex formulas into their simplest forms, creating more calculated variables as needed.

Of course, there are some cases where it's not possible to apply this rule. For example, **Demand** is calculated with this formula:

$$\textit{Demand = DemParA * DemParB \textasciicircum -Price}$$

This formula uses a product, an exponent and a change of sign: it's not possible to break down the formula. This is the case with many common scientific or domain-specific formulas. Table 2-2 shows some examples of how to apply the rule.

Table 2-2 Simplicity Rule Examples

Formulas to Avoid		Recommended Formulas	
Total Cost	*Fixed Cost + Unit Cost * Demand*	*Variable Cost*	*Unit Cost * Demand*
		Total Cost	*Fixed Cost + Variable Cost*
Payable Amount	*Total Amount * (1 + Sales Tax Percentage)*	*Tax Amount*	*Total Amount * Sales Tax Percentage*
		Payable Amount	*Total Amount + Tax Amount*
Rental Cost	*Number of Days * Daily Rate + IF(Total Distance > Number Days * Daily Allowance, (Total Distance – Number Days * Daily Allowance) * Distance Cost, 0)*	*Total Allowance*	*Number of Days * Daily Distance*
		Surplus Distance	*IF(Total Distance > Total Allowance, Total Distance – Total Allowance, 0)*
		Surplus Distance Cost	*Surplus Distance * Distance Cost*
		Duration Cost	*Number Days * Daily Rate*
		Rental Cost	*Duration Cost + Surplus Distance Cost*

The **Rental Cost** formula is represented in the left side of the table as one big formula. Whereas, to the right, it has been broken down into five very simple formulas, creating four new variables.

At a first glance, it's much easier to understand the set of short formulas on the right, each restricted to one operation, as opposed to decipher the complex formula on the left.

The same principle—breaking down a complex formula into several simple formulas to improve readers' comprehension—applies to the two diagrams shown in Figure 2-4 and Figure 2-5. Again, it's easier to explain the diagram of Figure 2-5 to others.

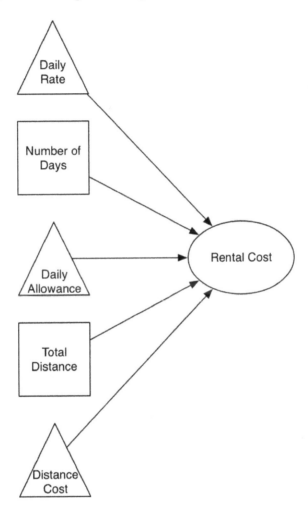

Figure 2-4 Diagram of a Complex Formula

Figure 2-5 shows a diagram with simple formulas, which facilitates its implementation as a spreadsheet. This deconstructed model gives a spreadsheet developer (either the original builder of the Formula Diagram, or another person) a clearer idea of how to build the physical model.

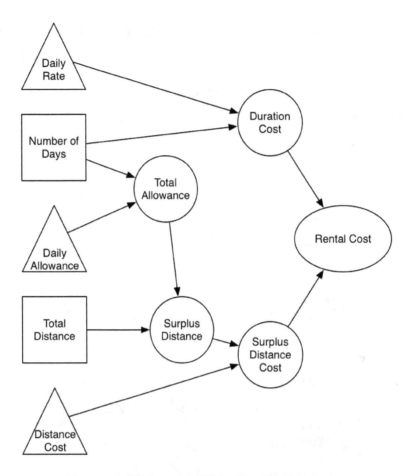

Figure 2-5 Diagram With Simple Formulas

Once again, looking at the two representations of **Rental Cost** in Excel, you can see an evident simplicity with broken down formulas. Figure 2-6 shows how the complex formula and the simple formulas would appear in a spreadsheet. Readers can quickly understand each calculation on the right, but would be hard pressed to verify the calculation on the left.

Daily Allowance	100	Daily Allowance	100
Number of Days	12	Number of Days	12
Total Distance	1,452	*Total Allowance*	*1,200*
Distance Cost	$0.36		
Daily Rate	$58.00	Total Distance	1,452
Rental Cost	*$948.36*	Total Allowance	1,200
		Surplus Distance	*252*
		Surplus Distance	252
		Distance Cost	$0.36
		Surplus Distance Cost	*$90.72*
		Daily Rate	$58.00
		Number of Days	12
		Duration Cost	*$696.00*
		Duration Cost	$696.00
		Surplus Distance Cost	$90.72
		Rental Cost	*$786.72*

Figure 2-6 Single Complex Formula vs. Many Simple Formulas

Breaking down a complex formula into many simple formulas also has the advantage of making errors easier to notice and correct. Figure 2-7 shows a spreadsheet that contains an error. Without comparing the numbers with those in Figure 2-6, can you find the error in the left side? You should find it easily in the right side.

Daily Distance	100		Daily Distance	100
Nb Days	12		Number of Days	12
Total Distance	1,452		**Total Allowance**	**1,200**
Distance Cost	0.36 $			
Daily Rate	58.00 $		Total Distance	1,452
Rental Cost	**948.36 $**		Total Allowance	1,200
			Surplus Distance	**252**
			Surplus Distance	252
			Distance Cost	0.36 $
			Surplus Dist Cost	**252.36 $**
			Daily Rate	58.00 $
			Number of Days	12
			Duration Cost	**696.00 $**
			Duration Cost	696.00 $
			Surplus Dist Cost	252.36 $
			Rental Cost	**948.36 $**

Figure 2-7 Spreadsheet With an Error

Let's take these basic principles of conceptual modelling, and apply them to a case study.

Case Study: Marco's Widgets

Marco is the owner of a widget plant. He specializes in manufacturing platinum widgets, which he sells to distributors worldwide. Each widget costs $180 to make, and Marco's plant has a fixed cost of $2,500,000 per year. In an attempt to increase his market share, Marco hired a marketing specialist to evaluate the potential demand for his product. She found that the relationship between demand (D) and average selling price (P) could be approximated by the following formula:

$$D = 376,000 \times 1.009^{-P}$$

This relationship is illustrated in Figure 2-8.

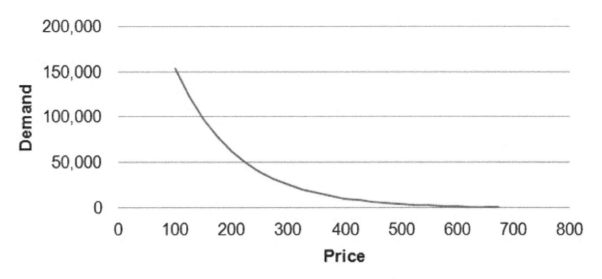

Figure 2-8 Relationship between Demand and Price

Marco has currently set the price of his widgets at $375, and he sells about 13,000 a year. This gives him an annual profit of less than $50,000. Marco wonders if he should raise his price to increase his profit. Over the next few chapters, we'll analyze his situation to determine the best strategy for optimizing profits.

Data Variables. These are variables whose values are set as constants by the spreadsheet user. In Marco's case, for example, you might define the first data variable as:

Fixed Costs = $250,0000

and the second data variable as:

Unit Cost = $180.

Following the advice of the market specialist, who determined the formula and its values, Marco set two Demand Function parameters: Demand Function Parameter A (***DemParA***) and Demand Function Parameter B (***DemParB***). The formulas for these are:

DemParA = 376,000

DemParB = 1.009

By using data variable names in formulas, rather than their values, you can avoid problematic formulas like:

*Commission = Sales * 7%*

Instead, prefer the pair of formulas:

Commission Rate = 7%

Commission = Sales * Commission Rate.

This allows users to change the commission rate by changing the value of a single cell, instead of having to individually modify every formula in which this value is used.

Input Variables. These are data variables whose values change regularly, as defined by spreadsheet users. In Marco's case, you can define Price as an input variable—since Marco wants to easily evaluate the impact of changing its value.

Calculated Variables. These are computed by formulas using data variables and other calculated variables—formulas that are well known to anyone familiar with the fields of accounting and finance. In Marco's case, you can define revenue with the formula:

Revenue = Demand * Price.

Output Variables. These are the results the model builder (and the user) want to see, the result of the whole process. An Output Variable is essentially a subtype of a Calculated Variable—one whose value is displayed in the spreadsheet's interface. In Marco's case, Profit is defined as an Output Variable.

Chapter 2 Overview

Here are the main points for you to remember from Chapter 2.

- Following the SSMI methodology, start the spreadsheet development process by creating the Formula Diagram and the Formula List.
- Classify your variables into types: Inputs, Data, Calculated Variables and Outputs.
- Following the Simplicity Rule, break down your formulas to just one operator.

In Chapter 3 and beyond, you'll use the Marco's Widgets case study to exercise your new skills.

Chapter 3   Developing a Simple Model

How to use this chapter

You should get more involved in this chapter. Take two sheets of paper and draw the Formula Diagram on one and write the Formula List on the other as you read through the chapter. It may seem pointless to do so, but there is a pedagogical value to do it: as you draw the diagram, you will be thinking about what you just read and you will ask yourself questions. I found that students who did that were quicker to understand the modelling steps. Allow about 30 minutes.

The Formula Diagram is designed to help you clearly visualize the variables in the Formula List. As you can see in Figure 3-7, each element of the Formula Diagram is shown in a specific way:

- **Data Variables** are represented by triangles,
- **Input Variables** are represented by squares,
- **Calculated Variables** are represented by circles,
- **Output Variables** are represented by ovals.

To indicate the relationships between variables—when one is part of the formula of another variable—the diagram uses arrows. Every calculated variable should have at least one incoming arrow.

Creating a Formula Diagram is a skill, and practice and experience are important. The following seven steps illustrate some basic techniques to help the process.

In the example shown in Figure 3-1, based again on Marco's situation, you can see that the input variable (**Price**) is on the left side of the diagram, and the output variable (**Profit**) is on the right side. This means you must now determine which variables and formulas—represented by the question mark—will eventually link the former to the latter. Identifying these is the creative task of the conceptual model.

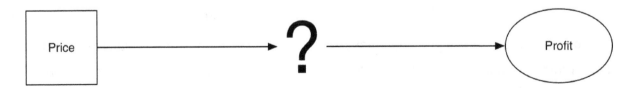

Figure 3-1 Input and Output Variables

These two variables are written in the formula list as shown below.

Variable	Type	Definition
Price	Input	*$375*
Profit	Output	?

Next, you must choose which data variables to add—such as these four.

Variable	Type	Definition
DemParA	Data	*376,000*
DemParB	Data	*1.009*
Fixed Cost	Data	*$2,500,000*
Unit Cost	Data	*$180*

These are shown in Figure 3-2.

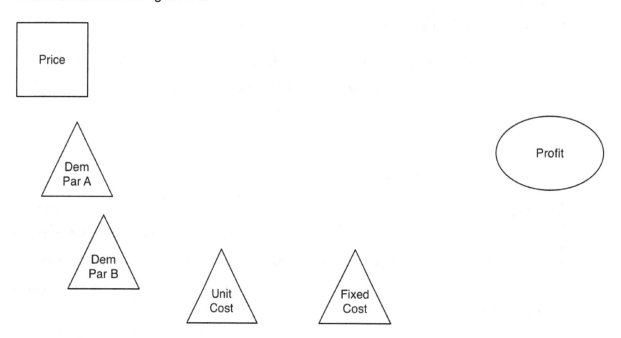

Figure 3-2 Introducing the Data Variables

Now comes the part where you need that creativity, experience and knowledge. The next step is to create the variables and formulas that will link the Input variable to the Output variable. There are two ways to accomplish this task: the **Forward Approach** and the **Backward Approach**.

If you use the **Forward Approach**, you consider the set of calculated variables and data variables in the diagram, and ask: "What new variable can I calculate with these?" As shown in Figure 3-3, the variables can be used to determine a new variable, one we'll call **Demand**. You can calculate this with the following formula.

Variable	Type	Definition
Demand	Calculated	*DemParA * DemParB^–Price*

When you draw arrows from each of the three variables used in the definition formula to the variable being defined, you see the diagram shown in Figure 3-3.

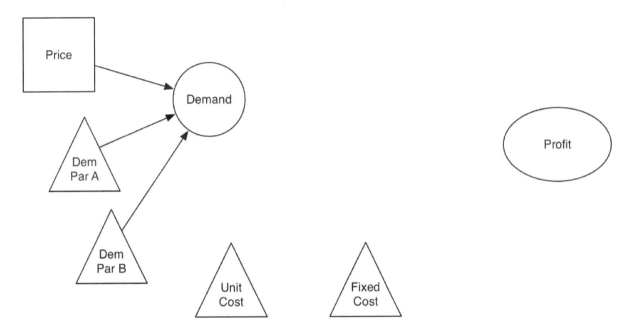

Figure 3-3 Defining Demand Using the Forward Approach

If you use the **Backward Approach**, it works a little differently. When you ask what you need to calculate the *Profit* variable, you might come up with this formula.

Variable	Type	Definition
Profit	Output	*Total Revenue – Total Cost*

Let's add the two new calculated variables to the Formula Diagram, shown in Figure 3-4.

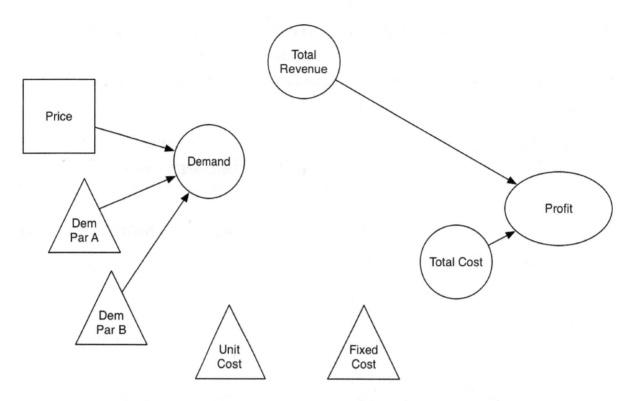

Figure 3-4 Defining Profit Using the Backward Approach

At this point, there are still isolated parts in the diagram. You must continue using either or both of the two approaches until you have all the formulas required. Continuing with the Backward Approach, you might ask: "How do I calculate the variable **Total Cost**?" The correct formula is shown below.

Variable	Type	Definition
Total Cost	Calculated	**Fixed Cost + Variable Cost**

With this information, you can add one new variable and two arrows, as illustrated in Figure 3-5.

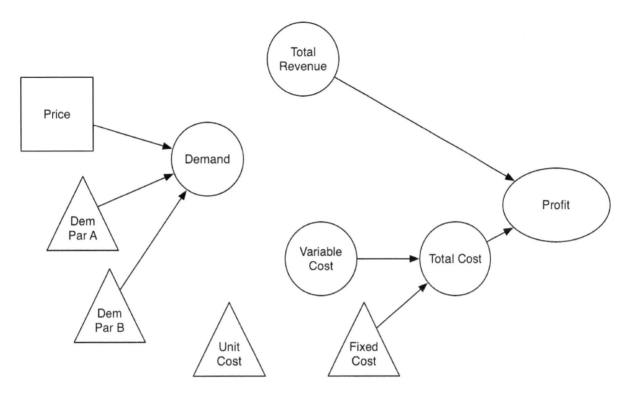

Figure 3-5 Defining Total Cost Using the Backward Approach

Next you must ask: "How do I calculate *Variable Cost*?" The answer is in the formula below.

Variable	Type	Definition
Variable Cost	Calculated	*Demand * Unit Cost*

This formula is represented in Figure 3-6.

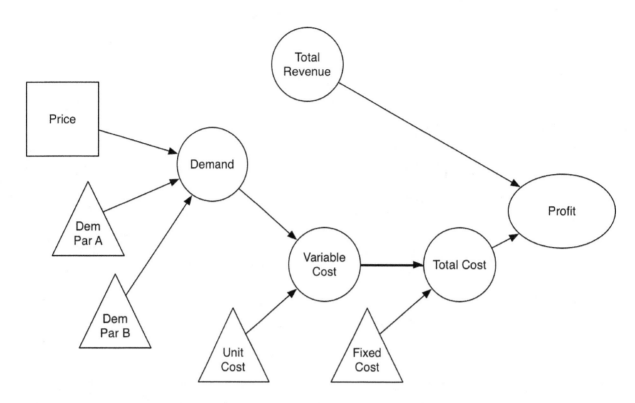

Figure 3-6 Defining Variable Cost Using the Backward Approach

Examining the diagram, you see that there is still one undefined variable. When you ask, "How do I calculate *Total Revenue*?", you get the following formula.

Variable	Type	Definition
Total Revenue	Calculated	*Demand * Price*

The final diagram is shown in Figure 3-7.

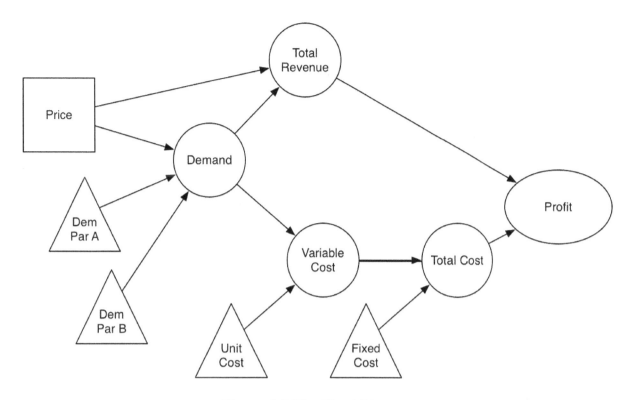

Figure 3-7 The Final Diagram

As you can see, the Formula Diagram above shows ten variables—some simple, some more complex. These should each be defined in a Formula List (such as the one presented in Table 3-1), which sets out their name, type and definition.

Table 3-1 Complete Formula List, Simple Model

Variable	Type	Definition
Price	Input	*$375*
Profit	Output	*Total Revenue – Total Cost*
DemParA	Data	*376,000*
DemParB	Data	*1.009*
Fixed Cost	Data	*$2,500,000*
Unit Cost	Data	*$180*
Demand	Calculated	*DemParA * DemParB^–Price*
Total Cost	Calculated	*Fixed Cost + Variable Cost*
Variable Cost	Calculated	*Demand * Unit Cost*
Total Revenue	Calculated	*Demand * Price*

Chapter 3 Overview

Here are the main points for you to remember from Chapter 3.

- Before you touch the spreadsheet software, it's important that you conceptualize your model from start to finish—from data to results, from input variables to output variables.

- In your Formula Diagram, draw the input variables (squares); the output variables (ovals); and the data variables (triangles). Link these with small formulas, creating calculated variables (circles) as you go along.

- Use either the Backward Approach, the Forward Approach, or a combination of the two.

- Every time you create a variable, you must add it to your Formula List.

Chapter 4 will show you how to enter these defined variables into your spreadsheet architecture. You'll also learn how to use the conceptual model.

Chapter 4   Implementing a Simple Model

How to use this chapter

As in the previous chapter, you should reproduce the spreadsheet implementation as you read through the section *Moving from Formula Diagram to Spreadsheet*. I show how to implement the first two variables in the **Model** sheet (Figure 4.9 and Figure 4.10) but you will have to work by yourself to implement the other variables and produce Figure 4.11. I suggest that you put a check mark next to the variables on the Formula Diagram and the Formula List as you implement them. Pay attention to the way we implement a subtraction. Allow about 30 minutes.

Finally, you get to actually create a spreadsheet! First, though, I want to talk about some development strategies, borrowed from best practices in the fields of information systems, software engineering and computer science. There are three of these, described in detail below.

- Using Three-Tier Architecture
- Using Range Names
- Using Modules

Using Three-Tier Architecture

This concept was developed to improve the performance and management of information systems. It consists of separating the three main aspects of systems; building them separately; and connecting them with the appropriate relationships.

These three parts are:

- the **interface**, the interactive tool that allows people to use the system;
- the **application**, the programs that implement the system's business logic;
- the **services**, the application's auxiliary services—such as getting data to and from a database, or accessing network resources.

In terms of spreadsheets, this three-tier architecture is achieved with the use of single-purpose Excel worksheets, each one having a specific task. The three basic sheets you'll always need are **Data**, **Model**, and **Interface**.

- The **Interface** sheet is where you enter the input and output variables. Spreadsheet users will work mainly in this sheet, assigning values to the input variables and examining the results obtained as output variables.

- The **Model** sheet is where you define the calculated variables, with blocks of simple formulas.

- The **Data** sheet is where you define all the data variables, including the inputs. These values can be either constants, or references to the Interface sheet, as long as you name them here. (As well, this sheet should not contain any formulas—except for unit changing or validation formulas that are not part of the model. This is explained in Chapter 11.)

The creation of these three sheets is illustrated in Figure 4-1.

Figure 4-1 Excel Sheet Names

For the simple model, you need use only these three basic worksheets to implement a Formula Diagram. However, as you develop more complex models, you'll need to use more than three sheets (though your architecture will always follow this basic pattern).

For a larger project, for example, you may have several data sheets, to make it easier for you to refresh their content when you need to. And if you have a particularly complex model, you may need more than one model sheet to make your sub-models easier to manage. Just make sure that you name the sheets appropriately.

Using Cell Names

The SSMI methodology uses names extensively to define variables. This is a concept that builds on the lessons learned from the early days of computer programming. In that long-gone era, programmers had to rely on numeric positions to indicate to the computer where in its memory was stored the data they wanted to work with. For example, an instruction to add together two numbers might be:

ADD 235,47,189

This told the computer to find the value located in "memory position 235," add it to the value in position 47, and place the result in position 189. This was an obvious source of error for programmers, who always had to remember that (for instance) position 235 contained the *Variable Cost*, position 47 the *Fixed Cost*, and position 189 the *Total Cost*. Since this system was both tedious and fallible, programming languages introduced the concept of naming memory positions. With this addition, the earlier instruction would now be written as:

ADD VARIABLECOST,FIXEDCOST,TOTALCOST

This made programs much easier to write, and to understand.

In Excel, rather than writing a reference to a cell coordinate like this:

=B274

you can refer to the cell by its name:

=Variable_Cost

Cell names tend to be a disputed spreadsheet topic, with only lukewarm acceptance from many users. This resistance is mostly due to a lack of understanding both of the benefits of names, and of how to use them properly. Many users pile up cell names in their formulas and functions, creating long and cumbersome strings. Others fail to realize that you can name entire rows or columns—a particularly useful feature in repeating sub-models, which are introduced in Chapter 5. The SSMI methodology encourages a robust engagement with using names, one that simplifies your task as a developer.

Using Modules

A **module**, a common concept in programming and software engineering, is a self-contained portion of a program with specific inputs, and instructions on how to manipulate those inputs to produce the desired output. An important characteristic of a module is that its instructions use only values that are already in its inputs (except in special well-controlled cases). This makes the module's results easy to verify, because they can be checked by testing with different input values.

In developing spreadsheets, SSMI emulates the module principle with a **block structure** where all new calculated variables are defined. This structure presents all the formula inputs with name references, and references to these cells, to calculate the new variable.

The name-referenced variables correspond to the values in the top part (above the line) of Excel's definition block; the instructions correspond to the formula in the bottom part of the block; and the formula output is the result produced by the formula. You can easily verify the result because all the values used by the formula are displayed by name. (This task is made even easier by Excel's cell-colouring feature.) Figure 4-2 shows an example of this block structure.

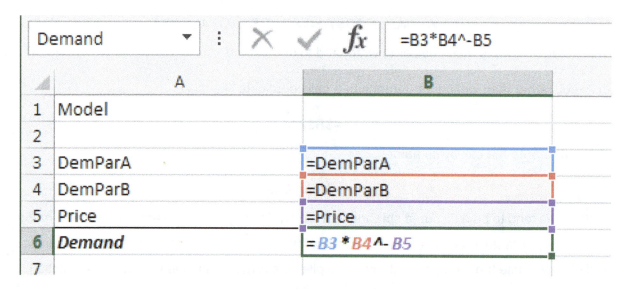

Figure 4-2 Implementing a Module in a Block Structure

Moving from Formula Diagram to Spreadsheet

If you have built your model properly, actually creating the spreadsheet is a relatively straightforward task. All the creative energy you put into the modelling (with the help of your Formula Diagram) means that now you just need to make sure you don't introduce any mechanical errors into the spreadsheet.

Let's create a spreadsheet using Figure 3-7 from Chapter 3, treating each type of variable as a separate step in the process:

- Step 1: **Data** Sheet
- Step 2: **Model** Sheet
- Step 3: **Interface** Sheet

To give you a quick visual guide, I've set all the references to Excel objects—everything you may need to observe or click in Excel—in an _underline and italic_ font. This means when you see something in that kind of type, you know it refers to a spreadsheet action.

Step 1: Data Sheet

In the **Data** sheet, enter the name of each data variable, including the inputs, in *Column A*; and enter its value in *Column B*, as illustrated in Figure 4-3. (As I indicated back in Chapter 2, all variable names are given here in **this font**.) Values should be formatted with the appropriate style for *percentage*, *currency*, *number*, etc., adjusted for your preferred *number of decimals*.

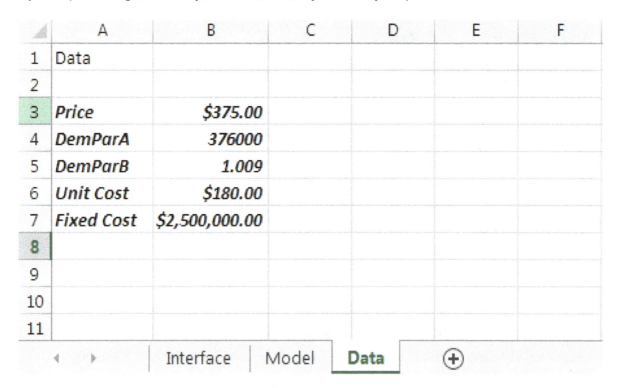

	A	B	C	D	E	F
1	Data					
2						
3	Price	$375.00				
4	DemParA	376000				
5	DemParB	1.009				
6	Unit Cost	$180.00				
7	Fixed Cost	$2,500,000.00				
8						
9						
10						
11						

Interface | Model | **Data** | +

Figure 4-3 Step 1, Defining the Data Variables

Then name the cells containing the values of the data variables by using the labels in *Column A*, as illustrated in Figure 4-4. (Naming cells is further described in Appendix A.)

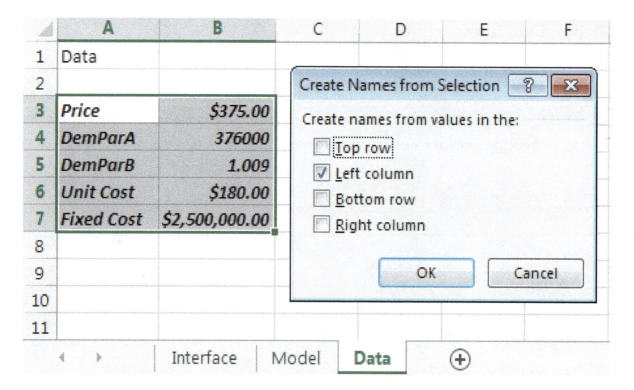

Figure 4-4 Step 1, Naming the Data Variables

Step 2: Model Sheet

In this step, you enter the definition of each variable and its associated formula. This presentation style allows you to validate the formulas visually, by looking at a printout.

As well as the definition formula, you also make extensive use of the reference formula—a simple formula that refers to the cell where a variable is defined. An example might be:

=Price

To create the definition formula, you enter the names of all the formula variables in a vertical block. Then you enter the reference formula next to each, as illustrated in Figure 4-5.

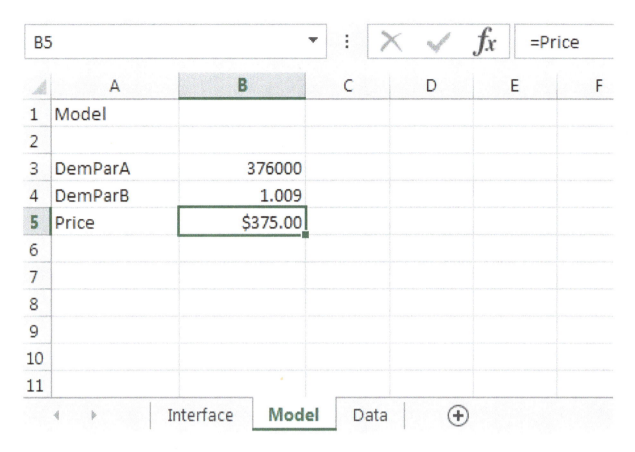

Figure 4-5 Step 2, Referencing the Variables Used In a Formula

Next, you enter the name of the new variable below all the others, along with the formula that defines it. The trick is to use only the values of the other cells, as illustrated in Figure 4-6.

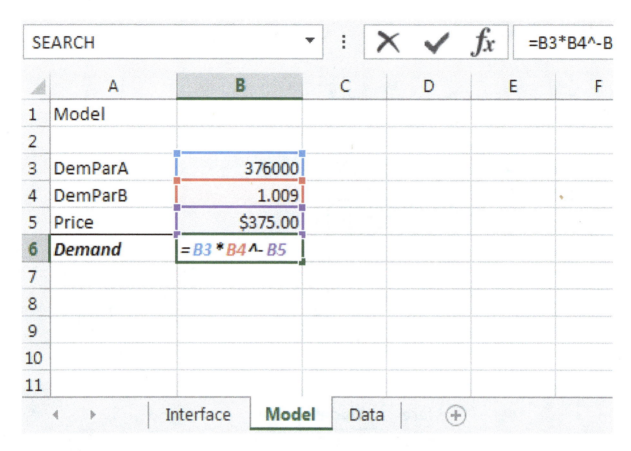

Figure 4-6 Step 2, Defining the Calculated Variable

Then you format the two cells as bold-italic, and assign a name to the cell that contains the definition formula—using its label in *Column A*, as illustrated in Figure 4-7.

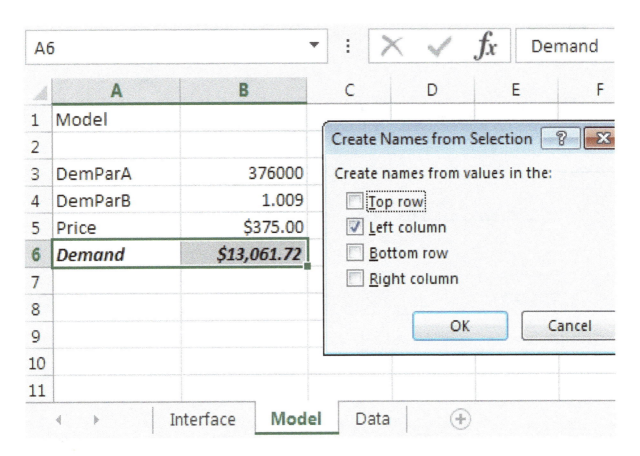

Figure 4-7 Step 2: Naming the Calculated Variable

To help readers visually distinguish the variables used in the formula from the result, it's helpful to insert a top border over the two selected cells—as shown in Figure 4-8.

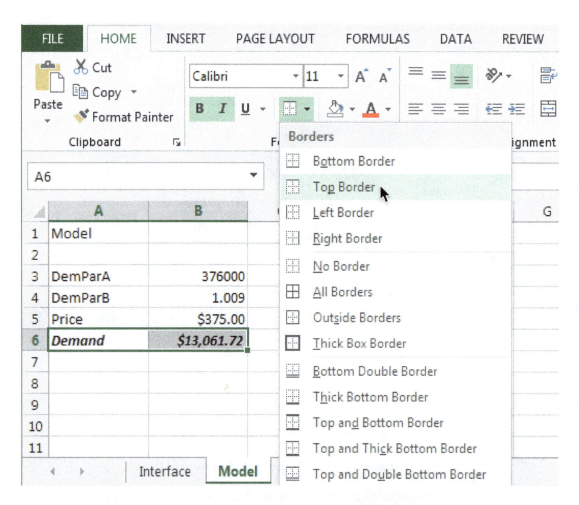

Figure 4-8 Step 2, Including a Border

Figure 4-9 shows the definition of the first calculated variable in formula view. The colour-coding allows you to easily see that the definition formula of _Cell B6_ refers to the three cells above it.

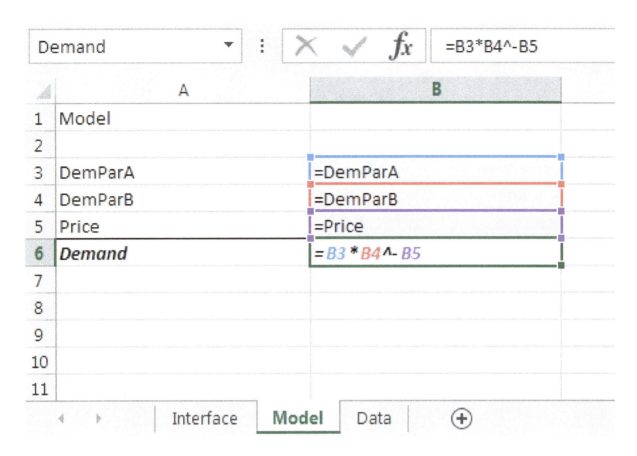

Figure 4-9 Step 2, Formula View of the First Block

Let's repeat this structure for the next calculated variable:

- enter the names of all the variables used in the formula in _Column A_;
- enter a reference formula next to each of these variables;
- enter the name of the variable you're defining;
- enter the variable's definition formula, using only the cells above it in the same block.

This process is shown in Figure 4-10.

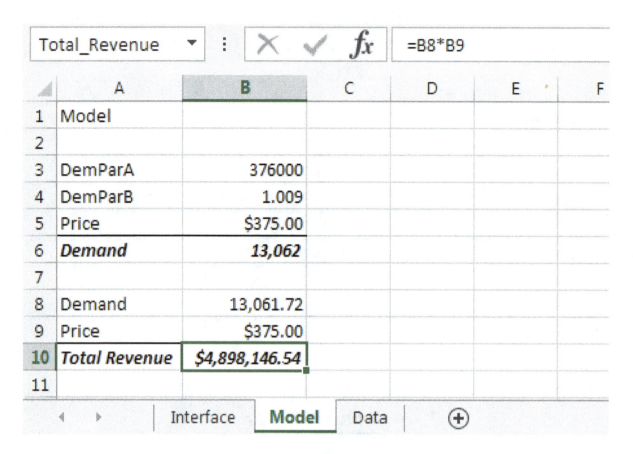

Figure 4-10 Step 2, Repeating the Block Structure

Continue to repeat this structure for all the variables defined by a formula: the calculated variables and the result variables. Figure 4-11 shows the finished model.

| Profit | ▼ ⋮ ✕ ✓ *fx* | =SUM(B20:B21) |

◢	A	B	C	D	E	F
1	Model					
2						
3	DemParA	376000				
4	DemParB	1.009				
5	Price	$375.00				
6	*Demand*	*13,062*				
7						
8	Demand	13,061.72				
9	Price	$375.00				
10	*Total Revenue*	*$4,898,146.54*				
11						
12	Demand	13,061.72				
13	Unit Cost	$180.00				
14	*Variable Cost*	*$2,351,110.34*				
15						
16	Fixed Cost	$2,500,000.00				
17	Variable Cost	$2,351,110.34				
18	*Total Cost*	*$4,851,110.34*				
19						
20	Total Revenue	$4,898,146.54				
21	Total Cost	-$4,851,110.34				
22	*Profit*	*$47,036.20*				

◄ ► | Interface | **Model** | Data | ⊕

Figure 4-11 Step 2, The Finished Model

Figure 4-12 shows the formula view. Note that the definition of **Profit** uses a sign-changing reference formula for **Total Cost**, and then adds it to **Total Revenue**.

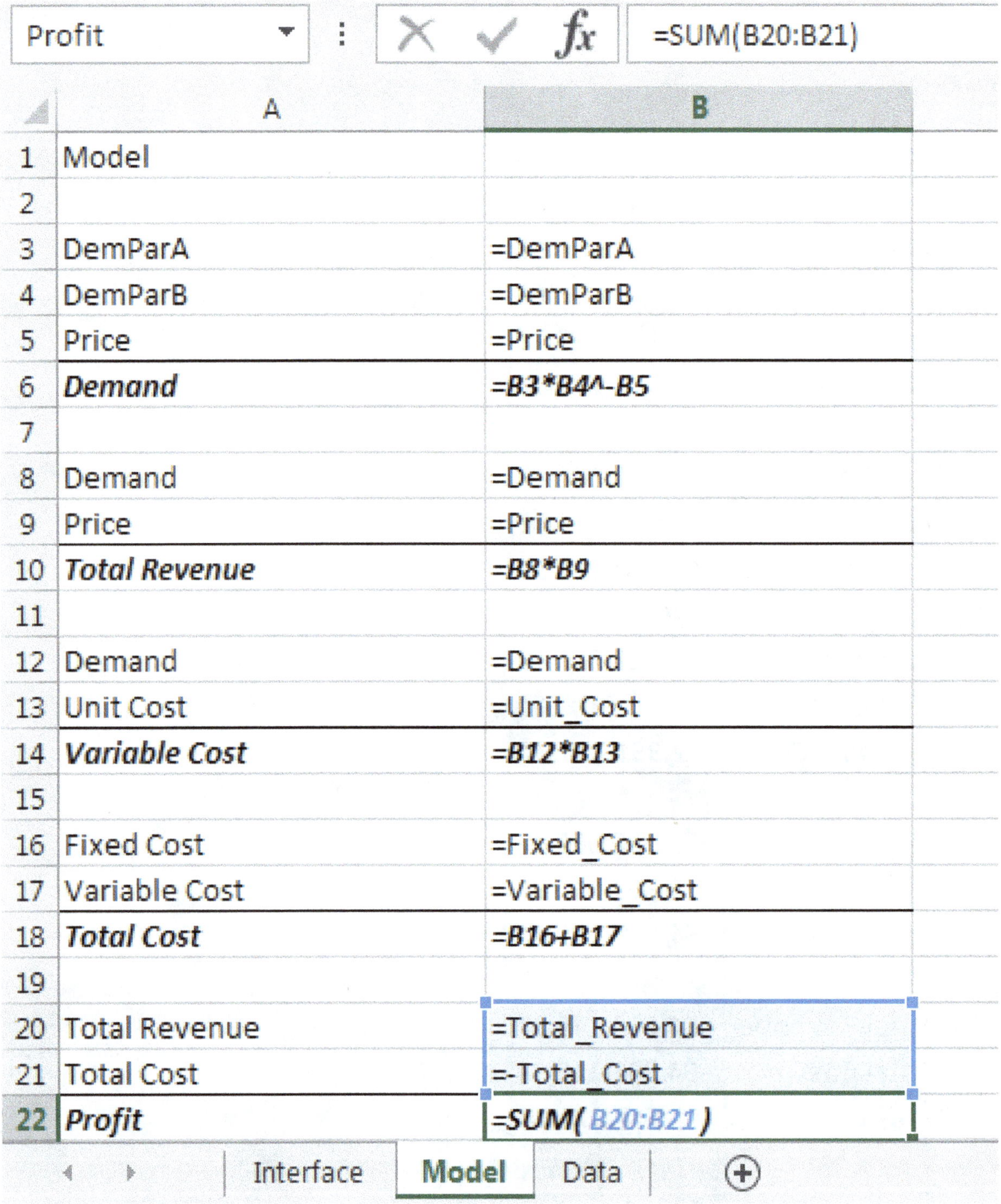

	A	B
Profit ▼ ⋮	✕ ✓ *fx*	=SUM(B20:B21)

	A	B
1	Model	
2		
3	DemParA	=DemParA
4	DemParB	=DemParB
5	Price	=Price
6	*Demand*	*=B3*B4^-B5*
7		
8	Demand	=Demand
9	Price	=Price
10	*Total Revenue*	*=B8*B9*
11		
12	Demand	=Demand
13	Unit Cost	=Unit_Cost
14	*Variable Cost*	*=B12*B13*
15		
16	Fixed Cost	=Fixed_Cost
17	Variable Cost	=Variable_Cost
18	*Total Cost*	*=B16+B17*
19		
20	Total Revenue	=Total_Revenue
21	Total Cost	=-Total_Cost
22	*Profit*	*=SUM(B20:B21)*

| ◄ ► | Interface | **Model** | Data | ⊕ |

Figure 4-12 Step 2, Formula View of the Completed Model Sheet

Since this way of representing a subtraction is a little unusual, I will explain it more fully. There are two ways to perform this operation. You can define the formula as either:

$$Z = X - Y$$

or you could define it as:

$$Z = X + -Y.$$

While these two formulas are mathematically identical, people tend to visualize them differently in a spreadsheet. Our minds readily recognize that numbers in a column are added together; but in a different format, readers must examine the formula closely to find its underlying logic.

Consider the formula that calculates the current balance of your bank account:

Ending Balance = Beginning Balance + Deposits – Withdrawals.

Figure 4-13 illustrates the two possible options for implementing this formula. The top block subtracts directly, while the bottom block uses a sign-changing reference formula **(=-Withdrawals)** and then a **SUM** function. When you need to share this material with others, the top block may take them a few seconds to understand; but the bottom block is quick and easy.

Ending_Balance ▼	⋮	✕	✓	*fx*	=SUM(B14:B16)

	A	B	C	D
8				
9	Beginning Balance	$12,573.00	=Beginning_Balance	
10	Deposits	$54,872.00	=Deposits	
11	Withdrawals	$57,152.00	=Withdrawals	
12	*Ending Balance*	*$10,293.00*	=B9+B10-B11	
13				
14	Beginning Balance	$12,573.00	=Beginning_Balance	
15	Deposits	$54,872.00	=Deposits	
16	Withdrawals	-$57,152.00	=-Withdrawals	
17	*Ending Balance*	*$10,293.00*	=SUM(B14:B16)	

Figure 4-13 Two Ways of Representing a Subtraction

Step 3: Interface Sheet

In the **Interface** sheet, you can enter the name of the input variables you need for the analysis. You can format this to your own preference, as long as all the values are properly referenced in the **Data** sheet. (This keeps all the variables handy in the same sheet, which is useful when documenting different scenarios—it prevents confusion about which values have been changed.) Figure 4-14 shows a simple **Interface** sheet. It can be set up to match any user's preferences—or an organization's, if they have their own formatting standards. A flexible **Interface** that refers to the **Model** sheet allows you to present information as you choose.

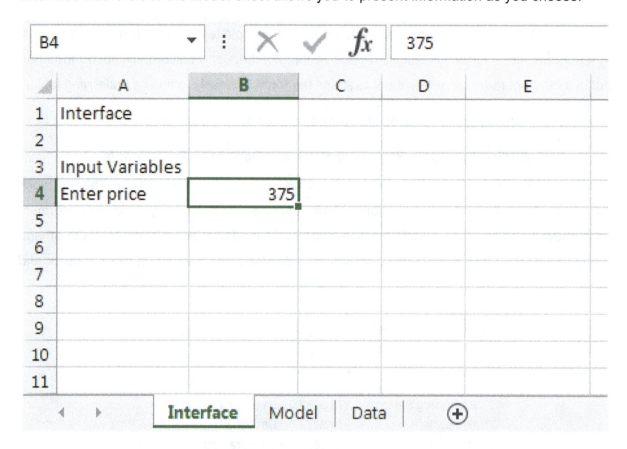

Figure 4-14 Step 3, Entering Input Values

You must therefore create the appropriate references in the **Data** sheet, as demonstrated in Figure 4-15. This allows you to manipulate the values in the **Interface** sheet without having to adjust any of the formulas in the model.

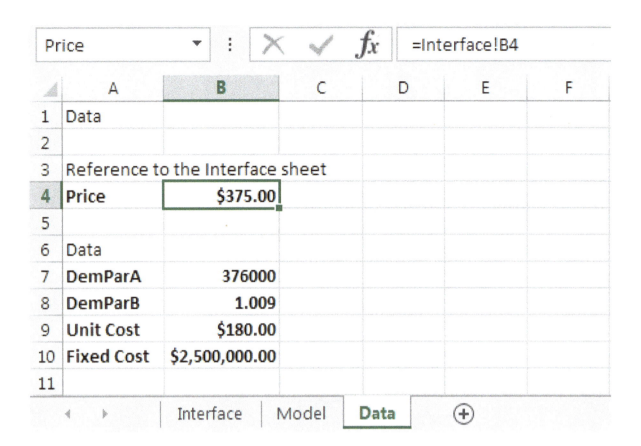

Figure 4-15 Step 3, Input Values for Data Sheet

You can now complete the **Interface** sheet by entering a reference formula next to each output variable. These are references to the variables defined in the **Model** sheet, as shown in Figure 4-16.

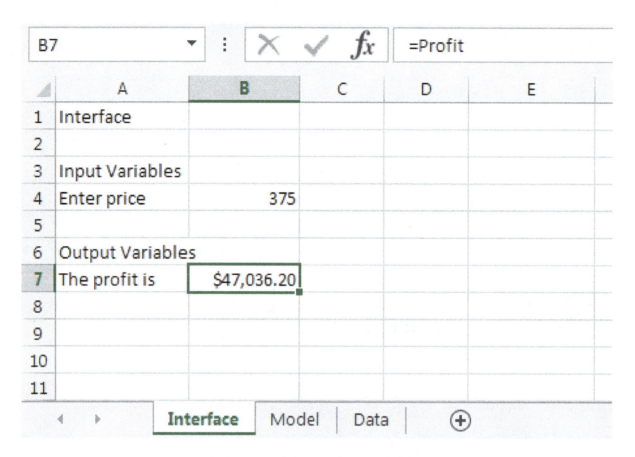

Figure 4-16 Step 3, References For Output Values

Finally, you can test your model by modifying the values of the input variables and observing how the output variables change. By increasing the price to $400, you see that the model predicts an unsatisfactory profit of -$203,089.72, as shown in Figure 4-17.

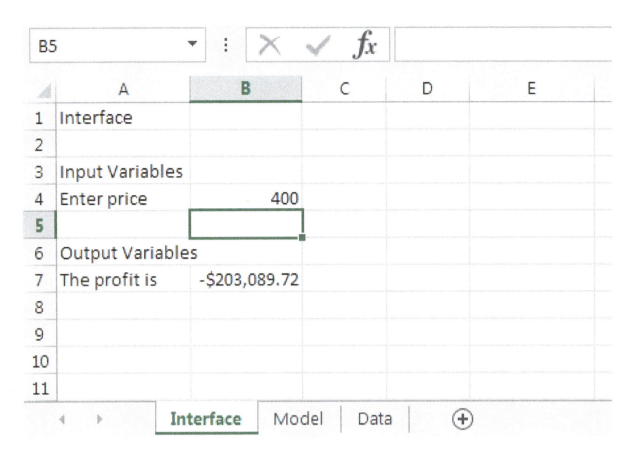

Figure 4-17 Analysis of a Single Scenario

Chapter 4 Overview

Here are the main points for you to remember from Chapter 4.

- In your spreadsheet, all the data variables—including the inputs—should be defined and grouped together in the **Data** sheet.

- Your **Data** sheet may contain either constants, or references to values entered in the **Interface** sheet.

- The **Model** sheet contains only formulas, and this is the only place formulas should appear. The only exceptions are the unit-changing formulas or validation formulas (described in Chapter 12) that may appear in the **Data** sheet.

- Variables are named where they are defined, either by a value (for a data variable) or by a formula (for a calculated variable).

Chapter 5 introduces you to the concept of the repeating sub-model.

Chapter 5   Developing a Repeating Sub-Model

How to use this chapter

Take out two sheets of paper again and, as you read through the Modelling Without a Repeating Sub-Model section, draw the Formula Diagram on one and write the Formula List on the other. Don't go as far as drawing Figure 5-9: it only serves to illustrate how big a diagram can become if you don't take advantage of the repeating sub-model concept. Modify your Formula Diagram as shown in Figure 5-10 by simply scratching out the South suffix of the variable names and drawing the dotted line box. On paper, you may have to draw the box as a non-rectangular shape to enclose the variables. Finally, modify your List of Formulas to reflect the changes in the variable names. Allow about one hour.

In some situations, you may find that sets of variables have similar formulas. The obvious solution seems to give them different names: **Profit Region A**, **Profit Region B** and **Profit Region C**, for example. But if you use the straightforward modelling technique shown earlier, the resulting model is unwieldy and difficult to modify. The simpler way is to identify variables and formulas that are similar, and group them into a **repeating sub-model**.

Let's take a look at how a repeating sub-model can reduce complexity. First, let's develop a model without this modelling technique. Then you can do it again with a simplified Formula Diagram.

In Marco's case, he sells his widgets in three different regions: South, East and North-West. He now wants a model that will show him his profit per region, as well as his total profit. In terms of demand for his product, he knows that the regions break down as follows:

- South: 48%
- East: 23%
- North-West: 29%.

Previously, Marco had used an across-the-board **Unit Cost** of $180. But now that he is considering regions, he can separate that figure into **Manufacturing Cost** and **Delivery Cost**: The **Manufacturing Cost** is $120, irrespective of region; and the **Delivery Cost** varies by region:

- $50 for the South region

- $80 for the East region
- $60 for the North-West region.

To calculate the profit for each of these regions, Marco must allocate the **Fixed Cost** to each region, with the same distribution as the demand.

Modelling Without a Repeating Sub-Model

Let's first look at how you would build the model with the methodology shown in Chapter 4. Beginning with the South region, you start the Formula Diagram with the six variables that are region-independent—that is, they do not depend on the specific regions. These variables are presented in the formula list below.

Variable	Type	Definition
Price	Input	*(To be set by user)*
DemParA	Data	*376,000*
DemParB	Data	*1,009*
Fixed Cost	Data	*$2,500,000*
Manufacturing Cost	Data	*$120*

Another important variable is **Demand**, which is defined with the following formula.

Variable	Type	Definition
Demand	Calculated	*DemParA * DemParB^–Price*

The diagram resulting from adding the region-independent variables is shown in Figure 5-1.

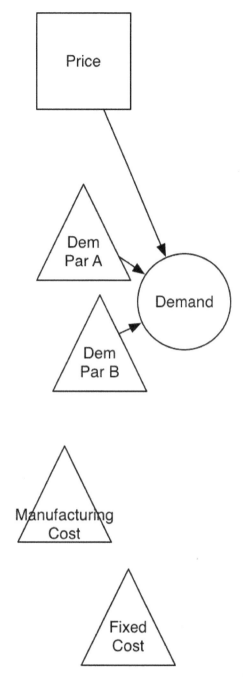

Figure 5-1 Region-Independent Variables

As you can now see, all the other variables from the previous model are region-dependent: that is, they change according to the region. These variables are added below in the formula list, which also allow you to define the **Profit South** formula.

Variable	Type	Definition
Profit South	Output	*Revenue South – Total Cost South*
Revenue South	Calculated	?
Total Cost South	Calculated	?
Variable Cost South	Calculated	?
Unit Cost South	Calculated	?

If you need new variables as you construct the model, add them as you go. Place these variables in the diagram, using formulas similar to the earlier ones. The diagram representing this is shown in Figure 5-2.

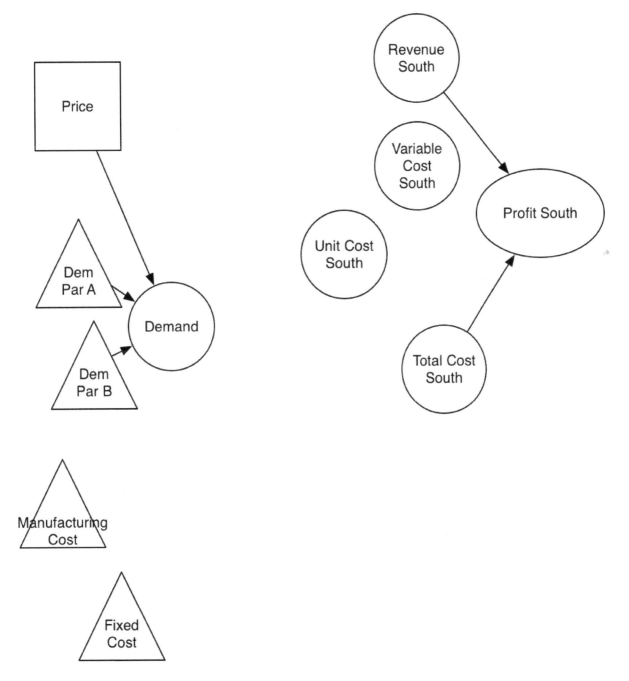

Figure 5-2 Region-Dependent Variables

Continuing to develop the model, you might ask: "How is *Revenue South* calculated?" You can use a formula similar to the original model by introducing a new calculated variable.

Variable	Type	Definition
Revenue South	Calculated	*Demand South * Price*

The diagram resulting from this is shown in Figure 5-3.

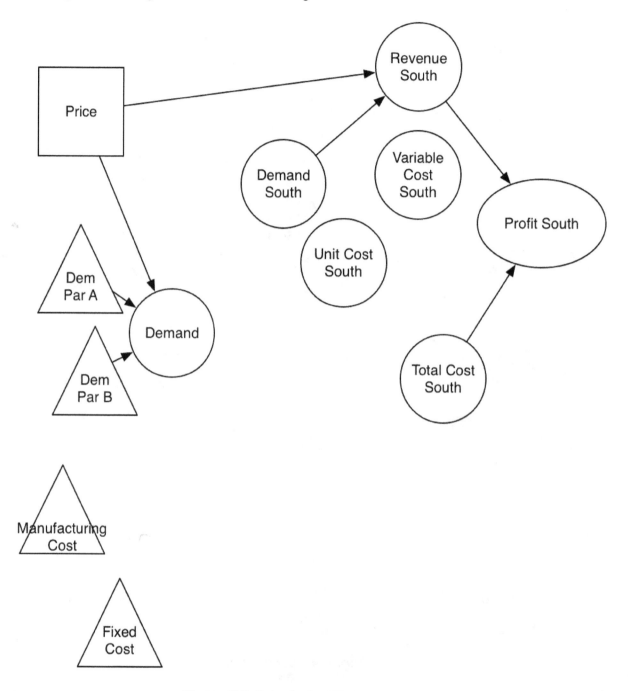

Figure 5-3 Calculating Revenue South

Now you can ask: "How is **Demand South** calculated?" Marco knows that 49% of **Demand** is in the South. This is one of three values that determine the distribution of **Demand**. So you create a new data variable called **Distribution South**. The formula is defined below.

Variable	Type	Definition
Revenue South	Calculated	*Demand * Distribution South*
Distribution South	Data	*49%*

The diagram resulting from this is shown in Figure 5-4.

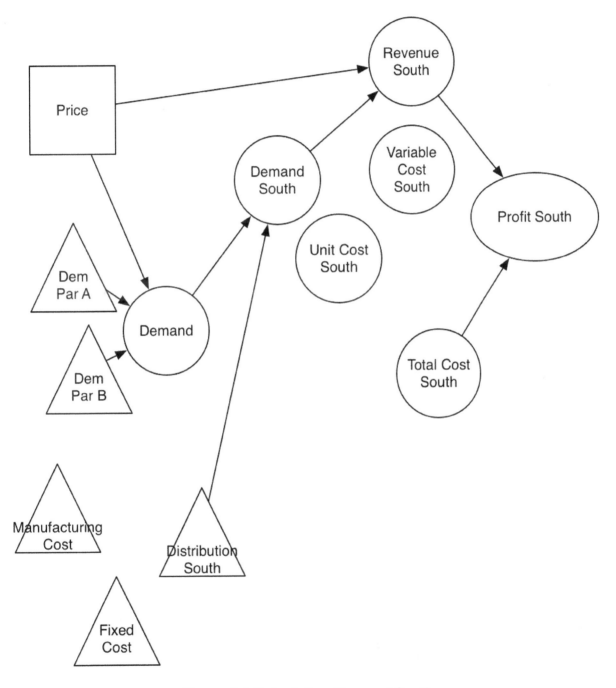

Figure 5-4 Calculating Demand South

You now have all the information you need to calculate the following formula.

Variable	Type	Definition
Variable Cost South	Calculated	*Demand * Unit Cost South*

The diagram calculating the *Variable Cost South* is shown in Figure 5-5.

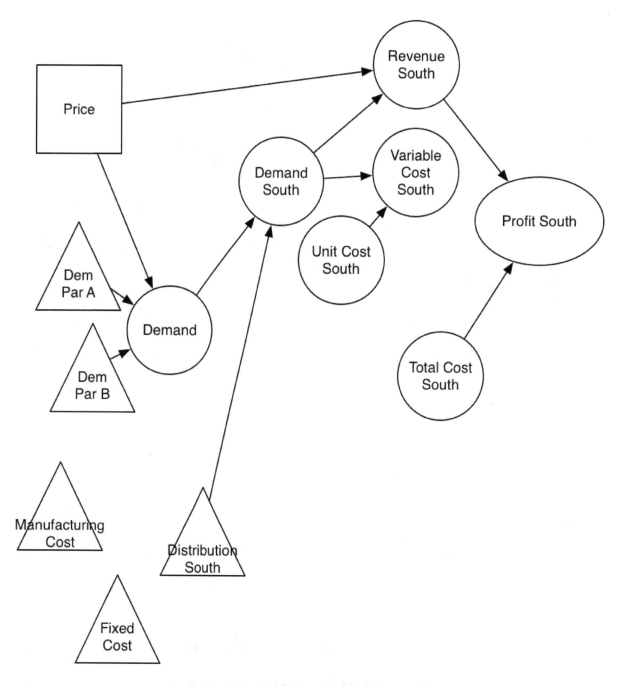

Figure 5-5 Calculating Variable Cost South

Now you need to calculate **Total Cost South**. You know that **Fixed Cost** covers all regions, so you need to create a new calculated variable to represent the fixed cost just for the South region. You might use this formula.

Variable	Type	Definition
Total Cost South	Calculated	*Fixed Cost South + Variable Cost South*

The diagram resulting from this is shown in Figure 5-6.

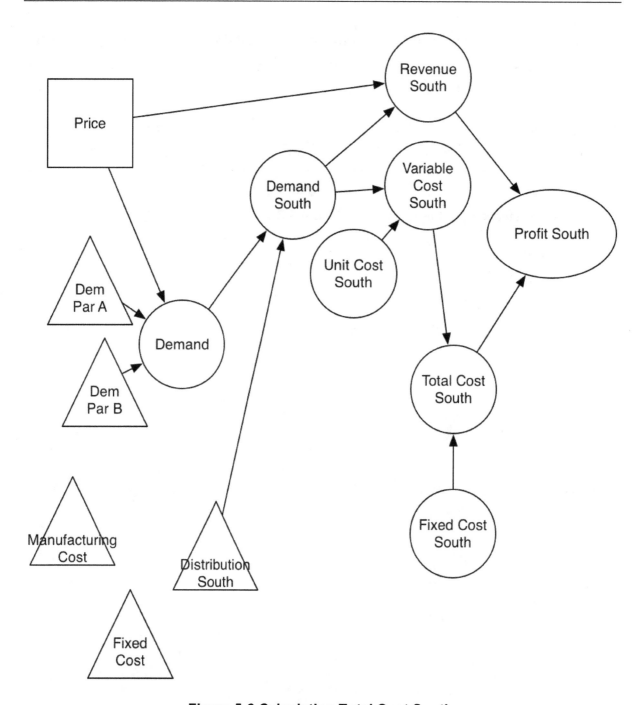

Figure 5-6 Calculating Total Cost South

When you consider how *Fixed Cost South* is calculated, you know that Marco's *Fixed Cost* is allocated to the different regions using the same data variables as the *Demand* allocation. This gives you the formula below.

Variable	Type	Definition
Fixed Cost South	Calculated	*Fixed Cost * Distribution South*

The diagram resulting from this is shown in Figure 5-7.

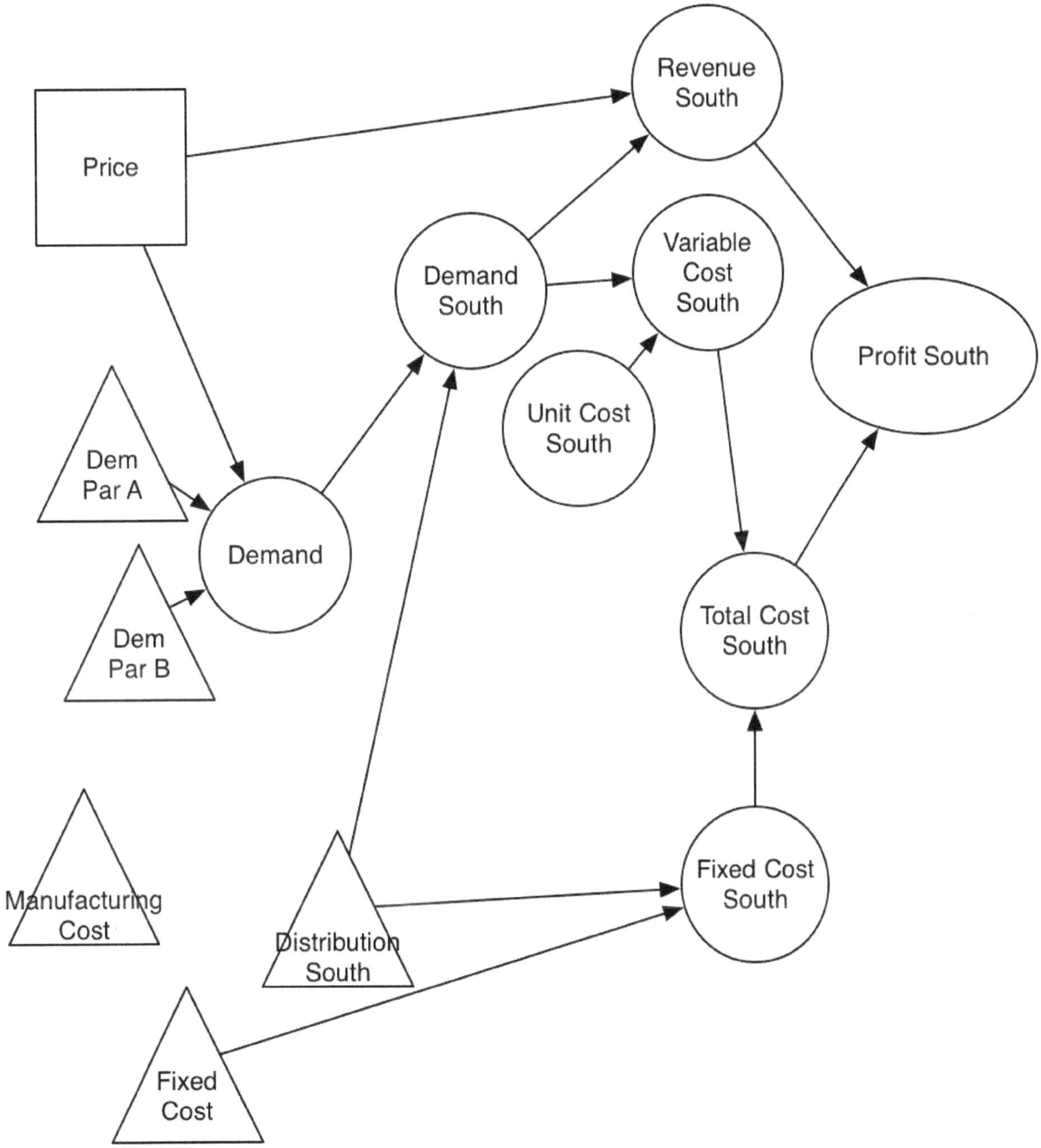

Figure 5-7 Calculating Fixed Cost South

Looking at the diagram, you see that *Unit Cost South* is not yet defined. You know that Marco's *Unit Cost* of each region is calculated from two values: *Manufacturing Cost*, which does not depend on the region, and *Delivery Cost*, which varies from one region to another. Introducing the new variable, you get the following formula.

Variable	Type	Definition
Unit Cost South	Calculated	*Manufacturing Cost + Delivery Cost South*

The diagram resulting from this is shown in Figure 5-8.

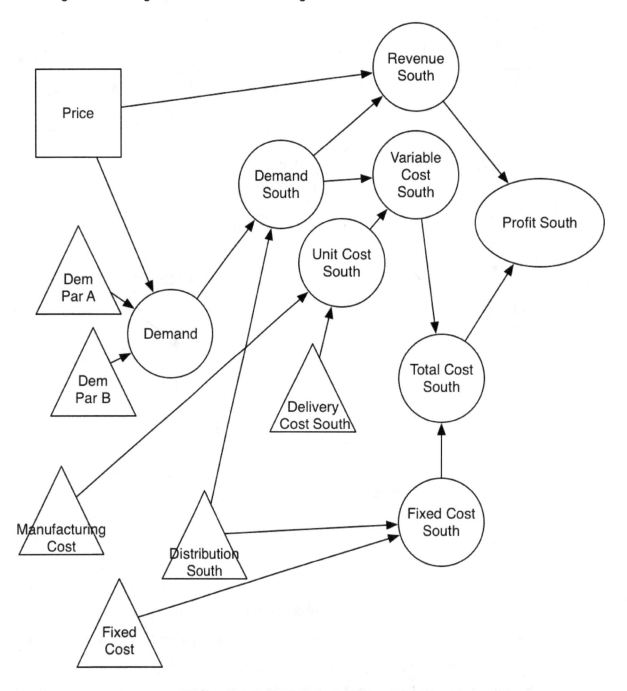

Figure 5-8 Calculating Unit Cost South

While completing this formula diagram, you have also filled out a list of variables and formulas that reflect the regional bias. This model is applicable specifically to selling widgets in the **South Region**. You can see this in Table 5-1.

Table 5-1 Formula List, Marco's Widgets South Region

Variable	Type	Definition
Price	Input	*(To be set by user)*
Profit South	Output	*Revenue South – Total Cost South*
DemParA	Data	*376,000*
DemParB	Data	*1,009*
Fixed Cost	Data	*$2,500,000*
Manufacturing Cost	Data	*$120*
Distribution South	Data	*49%*
Delivery Cost South	Data	*$50*
Demand	Calculated	*DemParA + DemParB^-Price*
Demand South	Calculated	*Demand * Distribution South*
Total Cost South	Calculated	*Fixed Cost South + Variable Cost South*
Fixed Cost South	Calculated	*Fixed Cost * Distribution South*
Variable Cost South	Calculated	*Demand South * Unit Cost South*
Unit Cost South	Calculated	*Manufacturing Cost + Delivery Cost South*
Revenue South	Calculated	*Demand South * Price*

If you leave the **South Region** and continue to the **East Region**, you notice that the variables and the formulas are similar. The only difference is that the variables use the suffix **East** instead of **South**. The same is true of the **North-West** region, with the suffix **N-W**. Without using a repeating sub-model, you would end up with an extremely complex Formula Diagram—as illustrated in Figure 5-9.

Figure 5-9 Formula Diagram Without a Repeating Sub-Model (Three Regions)

This model has obvious shortcomings. The most serious one is that it's very complicated, and not at all easy to understand. It also does not scale at all well. Imagine how incomprehensible it would become if you had to expand it to cover more regions, such as provinces, states or countries! Canada has 13 provinces and territories, India has 29 states, the USA has 50 states, France has 96 departments—so expanding the model to cover such divisions is completely infeasible.

Another shortcoming of this model is that any modifications (such as adding variables) would have to be repeated many times—and repetition always increases the risk of introducing errors. For these reasons, the repeating sub-model is easily the best solution.

Modelling With a Repeating Sub-Model

The advantage to using a repeating sub-model is that it greatly reduces complexity. The key to its effectiveness lies in naming the variables with suffixes. Instead of assigning one variable to each region, you instead use one variable to represent any region. This allows you to replace the variables **Delivery Cost South**, **Delivery Cost East** and **Delivery Cost N-W** by one sole repeating variable: **Delivery Cost**. Following Marco's calculation of regional delivery costs at the start of this chapter, you can define this variable as a set of three values: $50 (**South**), $80 (**East**) and $60 (**N-W**).

When you use the same variable name more than once, you need to somehow distinguish its different roles. For instance, if you use **Demand** to represent both a single value and multiple values, you might rename the two **Total Demand** and **Regional Demand**.

Applying the same principle to other repeating variables, you can redefine them as **Distribution**, **Regional Demand**, **Delivery Cost**, **Unit Cost**, **Revenue**, **Variable Cost**, **Regional Fixed Cost**, **Total Cost**, and **Profit**.

In your Formula Diagram, you represent a repeating sub-model by using a rectangle with a dotted border. In the top right-hand corner of the rectangle, enter the name of the repeating entity (in this case, **Region**). Then place all the region-dependent variables inside this sub-model rectangle, with all the other variables outside—as illustrated in Figure 5-10.

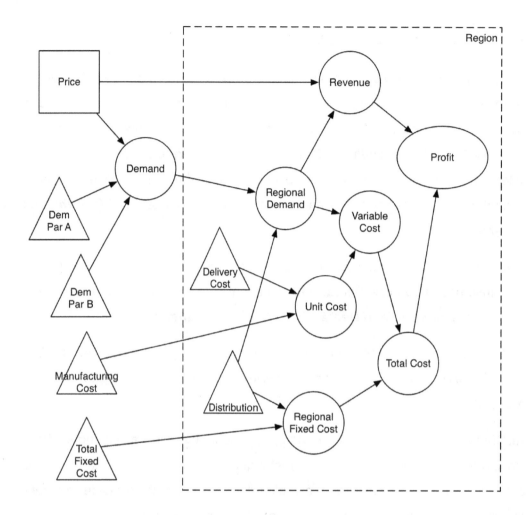

Figure 5-10 Formula Diagram With a Repeating Sub-Model

All the variables outside the rectangle represent single values, and all the variables inside the rectangle represent multiple values.

Conceptualizing Aggregate Functions

Looking at the current diagram, Marco notices that one important output is missing: the **Total Profit**. He wants this included in the result. To make the necessary adjustments, you should look at Figure 5-10, above, to see where you can insert that new variable.

The **Total Profit** is calculated by summing all the regional **Profits**. Because this new output is a single-value variable, it's outside of the rectangle. You should produce something similar to the adjusted Formula Diagram, in Figure 5-11.

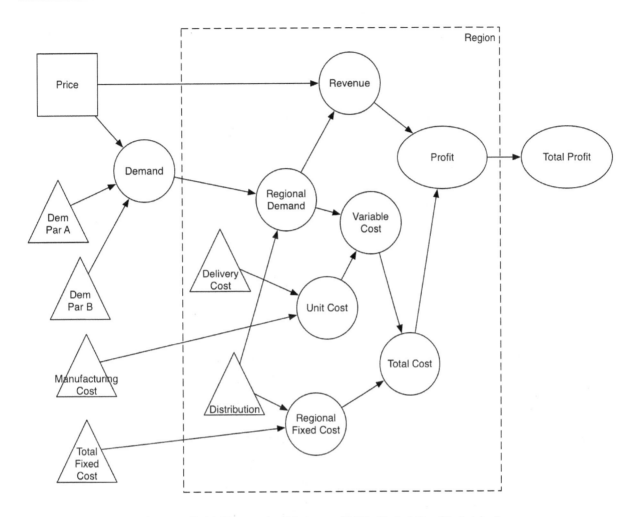

Figure 5-11 Formula Diagram With Total Profit Added

As mentioned, to calculate the **Total Profit** from the **Profit** of each region, remember that **Profit** (inside the repeating sub-model rectangle) represents a set of values; while the **Total Profit** variable (outside the rectangle) represents a single value. The function that calculates **Total Profit** must therefore take a set of values, and return a single value.

You may already be familiar with a few such Excel functions, called aggregate functions: **SUM**, **AVERAGE**, **MIN**, **MAX**, **VAR** (variance) and **STDEV** (standard deviation). Other more specialized functions, like **NPV** (Net Present Value) and **IRR** (Internal Rate of Return), are often used in finance and accounting models.

In this case, you can use the formula:

Total Profit = SUM(Profit).

This output variable represents total profit for all regions. As you go along building the Formula Diagram, it's important that you also add each and every variable to the Formula List. At this point, you should have a Formulas List like the following in Table 5-2.

Table 5-2 Formula List, Repeating Model

Variable	Type	Definition
Price	Input	*(To be set by user)*
Profit	Output, Region	*Revenue – Total Cost*
DemParA	Data	*376,000*
DemParB	Data	*1.009*
Fixed Cost	Data	*$2,500,000*
Manufacturing Cost	Data	*$120*
Distribution	Data, Region	*48%, 23%, 29%*
Delivery Cost	Data, Region	*$50, $80, $60*
Total Demand	Calculated	*DemParA * DemParB^–Price*
Regional Demand	Calculated, Region	*Total Demand * Distribution*
Total Cost	Calculated, Region	*Regional Fixed Cost + Variable Cost*
Regional Fixed Cost	Calculated, Region	*Fixed Cost * Distribution*
Variable Cost	Calculated, Region	*Regional Demand * Unit Cost*
Unit Cost	Calculated, Region	*Manufacturing Cost + Delivery Cost*
Revenue	Calculated, Region	*Regional Demand * Price*
Total Profit	Output	*SUM(Profit)*

Chapter 5 Overview

Here are the main points for you to remember from Chapter 5.

- The repeating sub-model is a way to simplify more complex models.
- Similar variables—with the same formula structure—can be grouped together.
- In the Formula Diagram, the repeating sub-model is represented by a dotted rectangle, with every variable inside it belonging to the repeating entity. The task of modifying the model is simplified by the fact that it doesn't repeat many times: any change only needs to be made once, no matter how many regions there are.

- Most importantly, increasing the number of regions does not change the model, or make it more complicated (though the spreadsheet will be bigger).

In Chapter 6, I'll show you a straightforward way to expand the model to accommodate more regions.

Chapter 6   Implementing a Repeating Sub-Model

How to use this chapter

You should reproduce the spreadsheet implementation as you read through the chapter. Pay attention to the fact that the model is first fully implemented in one column for one region, and then it's copied to the adjacent columns for the other regions. The last section is particularly interesting: it shows how easy it is to modify your spreadsheet to accommodate a change in your environment. Allow about one hour.

Like the simple model shown previously, the repeating sub-model follows a precise process. This time, rather than the basic three sheets described earlier, you'll need five sheets. The process of creating them again follows the three-tier architecture, as outlined below:

- Step 1: Two data sheets, one for the non-repeating data variables (**Data**) and one for the repeating data variables (**Data-Regions**);
- Step 2: Two model sheets, one for the definition formulas of all non-repeating calculated variables (**Model**), and the other for the definition formulas of all repeating variables (**Regions**);
- Step 3: The **Interface** sheet.

Step 1: The Data Sheets

Step 1.1: Non-Repeating Data Variables

You can define the single-value data variables and inputs as you did in Chapter 4: putting the labels in *Column A* and the values in *Column B*. As illustrated in Figure 6-1, name the single value data variables by selecting the labels and values you want, and clicking the *Create From Selection* icon of the *Formulas* ribbon.

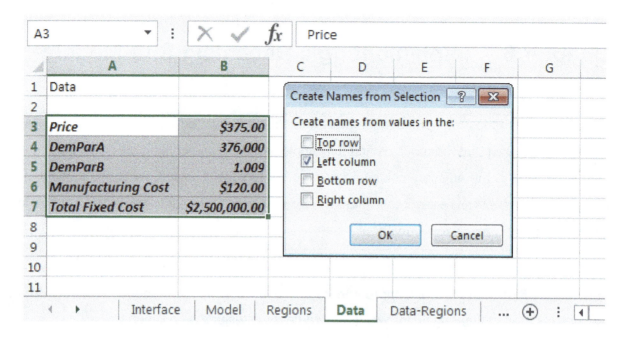

Figure 6-1 Step 1.1, Naming Single-Value Data Variables

Step 1.2: Repeating Data Variables

The multiple-value data variables need to be set up carefully. First you create a new sheet called **Data-Regions**. Next you enter the name of the repeating entity—***Region***, in this case—in *Column A*, along with the names of the data variables appearing in the repeating sub-model rectangle. Then, starting in *Column B*, you enter the values of the repeating entity and the data variables you have chosen, as illustrated in Figure 6-2.

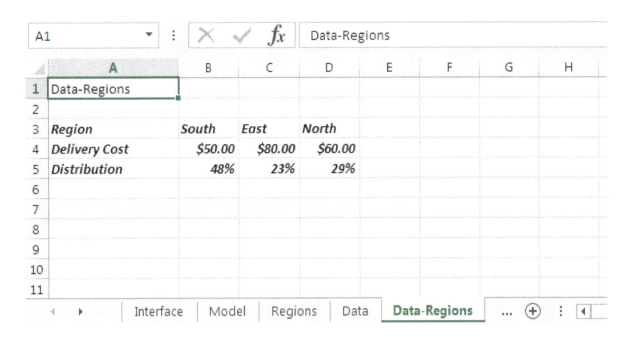

Figure 6-2 Step 1.2, Multiple-Value Data Variables

Finally, you name the repeating entity and the multiple-value data variables by selecting the entire rows containing all the labels, all the values, and all the blank cells that follow. To select entire rows, click on the *row number* on the left side of the spreadsheet. Then, in the *Create Names From Selection* dialog box, make sure that *Left column* is the only checkbox selected, as shown in Figure 6-3.

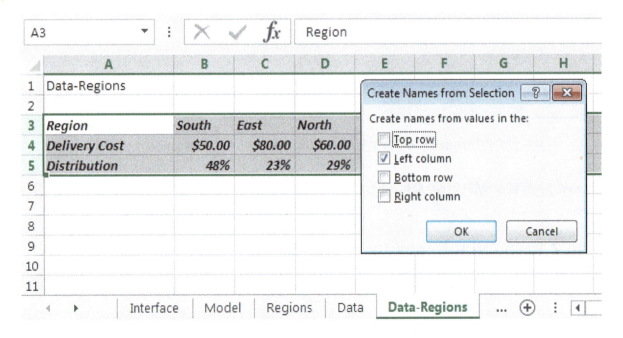

Figure 6-3 Step 1.2, Naming Multiple-Value Data Variables

At this point, you can verify that the names were created correctly by looking at the *Name Manager* window. In the example shown in Figure 6-4, you can see that **Delivery Cost** refers to *Row 4*, from B4 to XFD4, and is a set of three values followed by empty values. Naming the entire row, not just the range of values, makes it easier to update your spreadsheet in the future, such as adding new regions.

Naming the whole row this way allows you to add new regions quickly and easily, but you must be careful not to enter superfluous values into these rows. In this case, all the variables are named in the **Data** sheet or the **Data-Regions** sheet. This should always be the case for input variables and data variables.

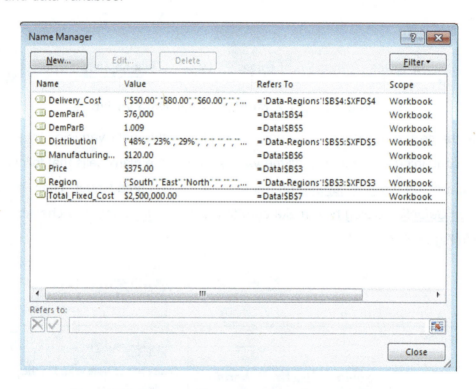

Figure 6-4 Step 1, Verifying Data Variable Names

Step 2: The Model Sheets

Step 2.1: The Non-Repeating Model Sheet

In the **Model** sheet, you need to enter the definition formulas of all calculated variables that are outside the repeating sub-model rectangle. In this case, there is only one: **Demand**. Figure 6-5 shows the block structure, with the defining variables above the line and the defined variable below. It also shows that *Cell B6* has been named **Total Demand**.

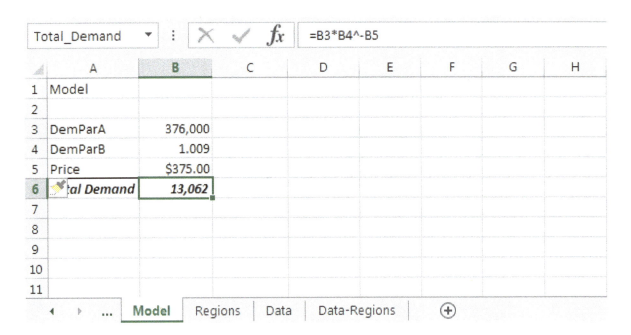

Figure 6-5 Step 2.1, The Model Sheet

Step 2.2: The Repeating Sub-Model Sheet

Implementing a repeating sub-model is done in two phases. The first addresses only one instance of the repeating item, following the usual block structure and variable-naming operations. The second phase copies the first model for all the other instances.

We start by identifying the region corresponding to the first column of the model. As shown in Figure 6-6, you enter the label **Region** in *Cell A3* and the formula **=Region** in *Cell B3*. It's important to start the model in the same column you used for the **Data-Region** sheet, or the reference formulas won't work properly.

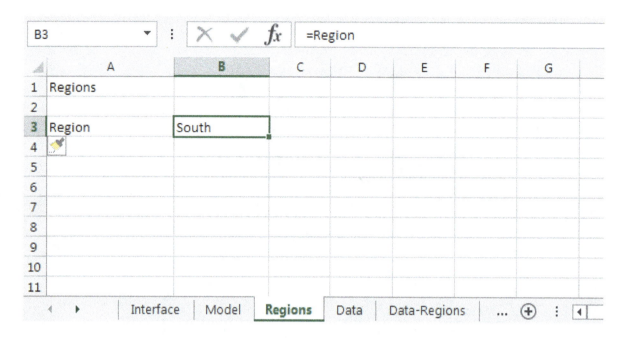

Figure 6-6 Step 2.2, Setting Up the Repeating Entity

In the block that defines *Regional Demand*, you first enter the variables that define it, along with their respective reference formulas. This is shown below in Figure 6-7.

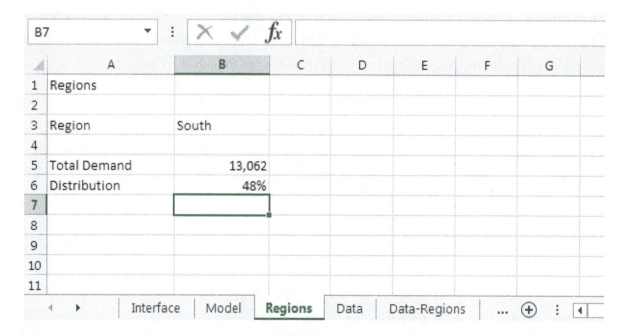

Figure 6-7 Step 2.2, First Block of the Regions Sheet

Next you enter the formula that defines *Regional Demand*, as shown in Figure 6-8.

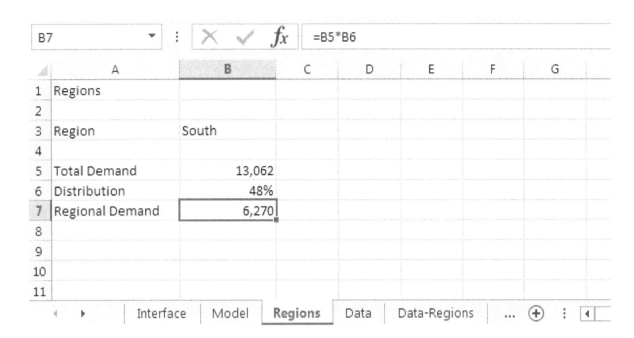

Figure 6-8 Step 2.2, Defining Regional Demand

Select the entire row of the variable you just defined—*Row 7*, in this case—and apply the bold-italic format. Insert a top border to create a visual separation from the defining variables, as shown in Figure 6-9.

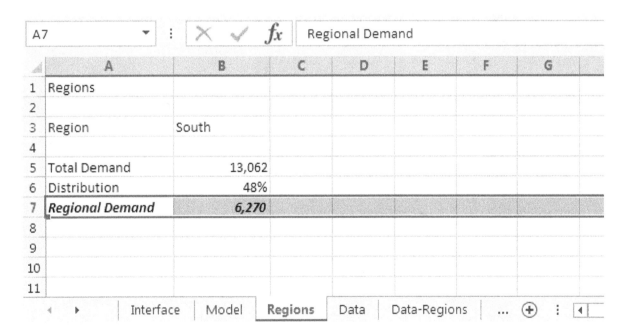

Figure 6-9 Step 2.2, Formatting the Variable Row

Name the variable row, as shown in Figure 6-10.

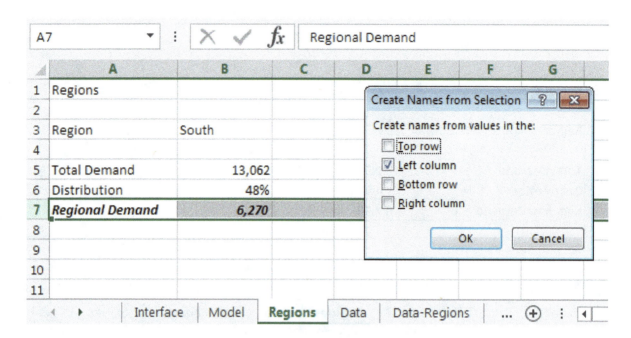

Figure 6-10 Step 2.2, Naming the Variable Row

Finally, Figure 6-11 shows the block structure for all the variables in the repeating sub-model.

	B31	▾	⋮	✕	✓	fx	=SUM(B29:B30)				

	A	B	C	D	E	F	G
1	Regions						
2							
3	Region	South					
4							
5	Total Demand	13,062					
6	Distribution	48%					
7	*Regional Demand*	*6,270*					
8							
9	Regional Demand	6,270					
10	Price	$375.00					
11	*Revenue*	*$2,351,110.34*					
12							
13	Manufacturing Cost	$120.00					
14	Delivery Cost	$50.00					
15	*Unit Cost*	*$170.00*					
16							
17	Regional Demand	6,270					
18	Unit Cost	$170.00					
19	*Variable Cost*	*$1,065,836.69*					
20							
21	Total Fixed Cost	$2,500,000.00					
22	Distribution	48%					
23	*Regional Fixed Cost*	*$1,200,000.00*					
24							
25	Regional Fixed Cost	$1,200,000.00					
26	Variable Cost	$1,065,836.69					
27	*Total Cost*	*$2,265,836.69*					
28							
29	Revenue	$2,351,110.34					
30	Total Cost	-$2,265,836.69					
31	*Profit*	*$85,273.65*					
32							

◀ ▶	Interface	Model	**Regions**	Data	Data-Regions	... ⊕ ⋮ ◀

Figure 6-11 Step 2.2, Complete Model for One Region

Once you have completed the model for one region, you can copy it to the other regions. You do this by selecting *Column B* and using the *copy handle* (the little square in the top-right corner of *Cell B1*, as shown in Figure 6-12).

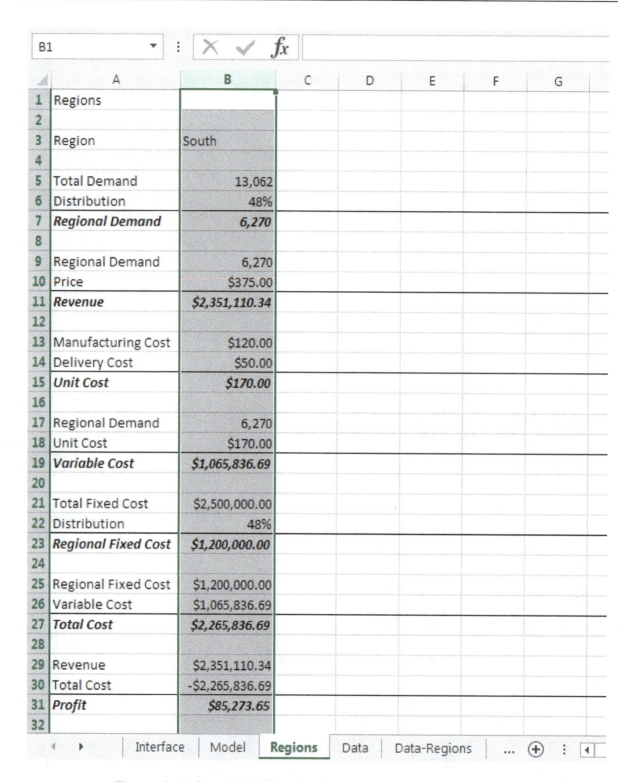

Figure 6-12 Step 2.2, Selecting the Full Model of One Region

To copy the model, just drag the _copy handle_ two columns to the right, and release. The result is shown in Figure 6-13.

B1

	A	B	C	D	E	F
1	Regions					
2						
3	Region	South	East	North		
4						
5	Total Demand	13,062	13,062	13,062		
6	Distribution	48%	23%	29%		
7	*Regional Demand*	*6,270*	*3,004*	*3,788*		
8						
9	Regional Demand	6,270	3,004	3,788		
10	Price	$375.00	$375.00	$375.00		
11	*Revenue*	*$2,351,110.34*	*$1,126,573.70*	*$1,420,462.50*		
12						
13	Manufacturing Cost	$120.00	$120.00	$120.00		
14	Delivery Cost	$50.00	$80.00	$60.00		
15	*Unit Cost*	*$170.00*	*$200.00*	*$180.00*		
16						
17	Regional Demand	6,270	3,004	3,788		
18	Unit Cost	$170.00	$200.00	$180.00		
19	*Variable Cost*	*$1,065,836.69*	*$600,839.31*	*$681,822.00*		
20						
21	Total Fixed Cost	$2,500,000.00	$2,500,000.00	$2,500,000.00		
22	Distribution	48%	23%	29%		
23	*Regional Fixed Cost*	*$1,200,000.00*	*$575,000.00*	*$725,000.00*		
24						
25	Regional Fixed Cost	$1,200,000.00	$575,000.00	$725,000.00		
26	Variable Cost	$1,065,836.69	$600,839.31	$681,822.00		
27	*Total Cost*	*$2,265,836.69*	*$1,175,839.31*	*$1,406,822.00*		
28						
29	Revenue	$2,351,110.34	$1,126,573.70	$1,420,462.50		
30	Total Cost	-$2,265,836.69	-$1,175,839.31	-$1,406,822.00		
31	*Profit*	*$85,273.65*	*-$49,265.60*	*$13,640.50*		
32						

Interface | Model | **Regions** | Data | Data-Regions

Figure 6-13 Step 2.2, Copying the Full Model

Step 3: The Interface Sheet

The final step is setting up the interface to suit your preference, as shown in Figure 6-14.

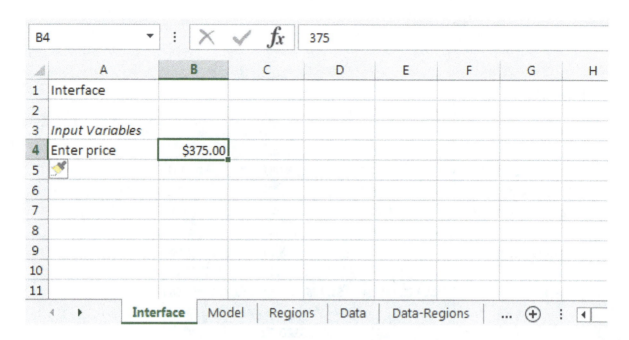

Figure 6-14 Step 3, Entering Input Values

Once again, it's important that all inputs that appear on this sheet are referenced from the **Data** sheet. This means that though their values are entered in the **Interface** sheet, they remain defined in the **Data** sheet—as shown in Figure 6-15.

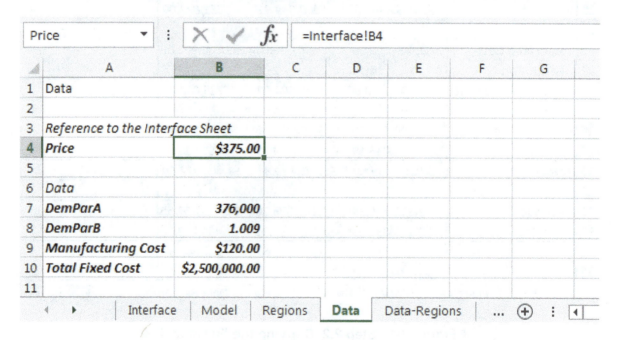

Figure 6-15 Step 3, Referencing Input Values in the Data Sheet

Next, in the **Interface** sheet, enter the references to the output variables in _Column B_: the reference formulas for **Region**, and the **Profit** output variables, as illustrated in Figure 6-16.

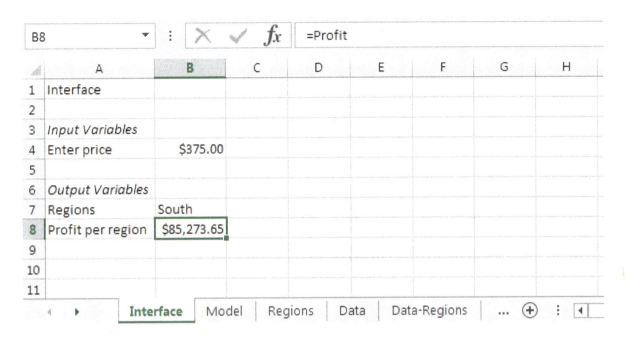

Figure 6-16 Step 3, Reference Formulas For One Region

Finally, copy the formulas by dragging the copy handle to extend the results to all the regions. The result is shown in Figure 6-17.

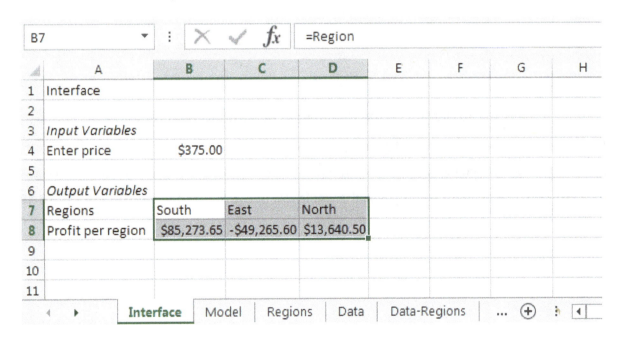

Figure 6-17 Step 3, Output Variables For All Regions

Implementing Aggregate Functions

Now you need to modify the spreadsheet to take into account the output variable that aggregates all the regional profits. Since **Total Profit** is a non-repeating variable, it needs to be defined in the model sheet—even though it also uses a repeating variable in its calculation. First you set up the usual block structure, with the references in the top part, as shown in Figure 6-18.

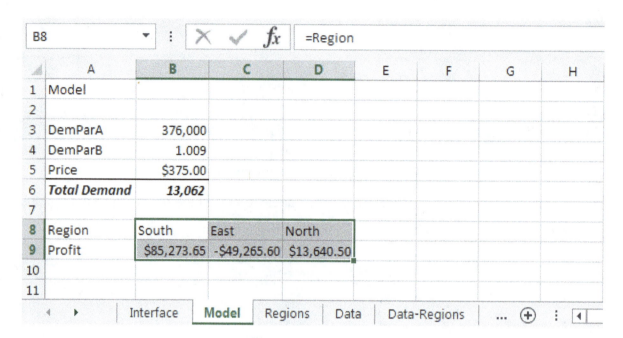

Figure 6-18 Setting up the Calculation of a Non-Repeating Variable

Next, enter the formula in _Cell B10_ as the sum of the whole row above it. To differentiate the repeating variable from the single-value variable, you can insert a border over the whole row—as a visual indication that _Cell B10_ uses the whole row above it. You can see this in Figure 6-19.

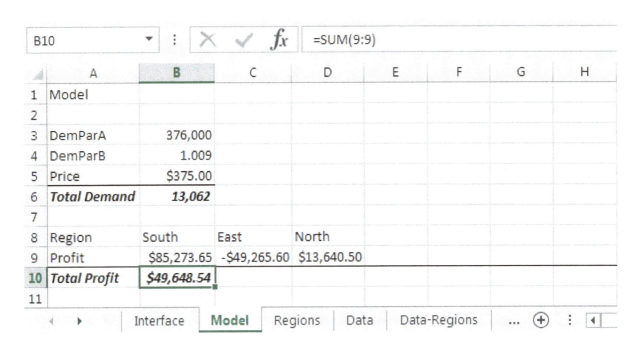

Figure 6-19 Aggregate Formula for Defining a Non-Repeating Variable

As shown in Figure 6-20, you name the single _Cell B10_ rather than the whole _Row 10_.

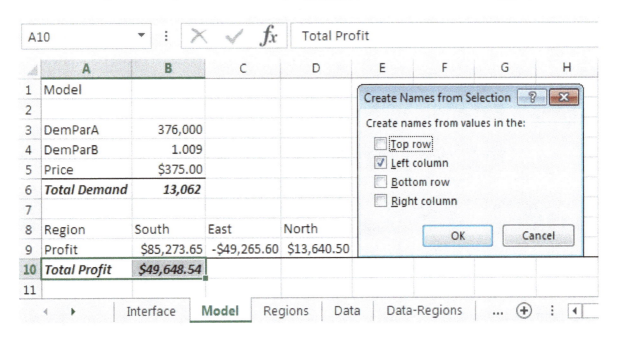

Figure 6-20 Naming a Variable that Uses an Aggregate Function

Since **Total Profit** is an output variable, write the reference formula in the **Interface** sheet, as illustrated in Figure 6-21.

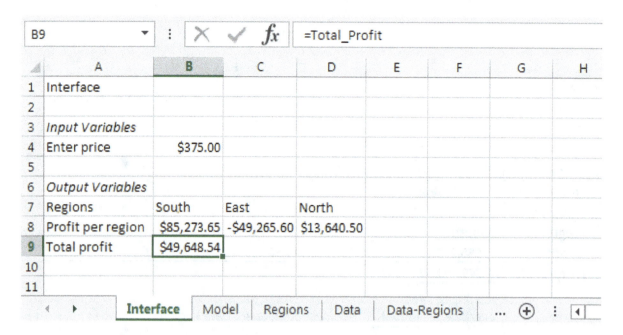

Figure 6-21 Referencing a New Output Variable

The repeating model is now complete. Like the simple model developed earlier, this tool allows you to easily and mechanically create a spreadsheet from a conceptual model. The exercise below also demonstrates the simplicity of modifying a spreadsheet developed from the SSMI methodology.

Exercise: Expanding Regions

Because of the size of the **South** region, Marco decides to split it in two. The new regions, called **Upper South** and **Lower South**, represent 30% and 18% of demand respectively; and their delivery costs are $62 and $30. How might you modify Marco's Formula Diagram, Formula List and spreadsheet to reflect this change?

Once you look at the problem, you realize that the Formula Diagram does not in fact change. You only need to modify the set of values for the Distribution and Delivery Cost data variables in the Formula List.

Variable	Type	Definition
Distribution	Data, Region	*30%, 18%, 23%, 29%*
Delivery Cost	Data, Region	*$62, $30, $80, $60*

Then you modify your spreadsheet to take this change into consideration. In the **Data** sheet, enter the following information:

- change the name of the **South** region to **Upper South**,
- change the values **$50** to **$62**, and **48%** to **30%**,
- insert a column after _Column B_,
- in the empty _Column C_, add the values **Lower South**, **$30** and **18%** for the data variables **Region**, **Delivery Cost** and **Distribution**.

These adjustments are shown in Figure 6-22.

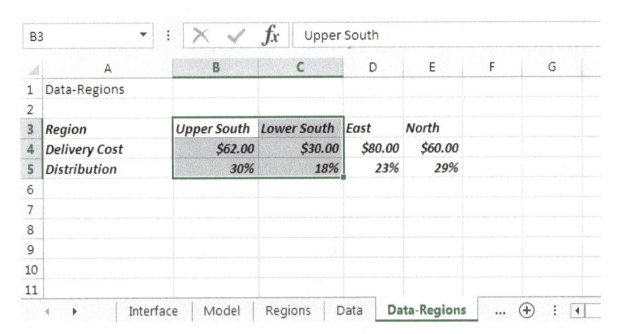

Figure 6-22 Adding a New Region to the Data Sheet

Next, copy the formulas of _Column D_ to _Column E_ in all the sheets where the repeating entity appears, in this case: the **Regions** sheet (Figure 6-23), the **Model** sheet (Figure 6-24) and the **Interface** sheet (Figure 6-25). You can see the new region in Figure 6-23, where there are now four instances of the repeating entity.

| B1 | | ▼ | ⋮ | ✕ ✓ *fx* | | | |

◢	A	B	C	D	E	F
1	Regions					
2						
3	Region	Upper South	Lower South	East	North	
4						
5	Total Demand	13,062	13,062	13,062	13,062	
6	Distribution	30%	18%	23%	29%	
7	*Regional Demand*	*3,919*	*2,351*	*3,004*	*3,788*	
8						
9	Regional Demand	3,919	2,351	3,004	3,788	
10	Price	$375.00	$375.00	$375.00	$375.00	
11	*Revenue*	*$1,469,443.96*	*$881,666.38*	*$1,126,573.70*	*$1,420,462.50*	
12						
13	Manufacturing Cost	$120.00	$120.00	$120.00	$120.00	
14	Delivery Cost	$62.00	$30.00	$80.00	$60.00	
15	*Unit Cost*	*$182.00*	*$150.00*	*$200.00*	*$180.00*	
16						
17	Regional Demand	3,919	2,351	3,004	3,788	
18	Unit Cost	$182.00	$150.00	$200.00	$180.00	
19	*Variable Cost*	*$713,170.14*	*$352,666.55*	*$600,839.31*	*$681,822.00*	
20						
21	Total Fixed Cost	$2,500,000.00	$2,500,000.00	$2,500,000.00	$2,500,000.00	
22	Distribution	30%	18%	23%	29%	
23	*Regional Fixed Cost*	*$750,000.00*	*$450,000.00*	*$575,000.00*	*$725,000.00*	
24						
25	Regional Fixed Cost	$750,000.00	$450,000.00	$575,000.00	$725,000.00	
26	Variable Cost	$713,170.14	$352,666.55	$600,839.31	$681,822.00	
27	*Total Cost*	*$1,463,170.14*	*$802,666.55*	*$1,175,839.31*	*$1,406,822.00*	
28						
29	Revenue	$1,469,443.96	$881,666.38	$1,126,573.70	$1,420,462.50	
30	Total Cost	-$1,463,170.14	-$802,666.55	-$1,175,839.31	-$1,406,822.00	
31	*Profit*	*$6,273.83*	*$78,999.83*	*-$49,265.60*	*$13,640.50*	
32						

Interface | Model | **Regions** | Data | Data-Regions | ... ⊕ ⋮ ◀

Figure 6-23 Adding a New Region to the Regions Sheet

Again, in Figure 6-24, you can see the **Model** sheet with a new region. The four regions are used to calculate **Total Profit**.

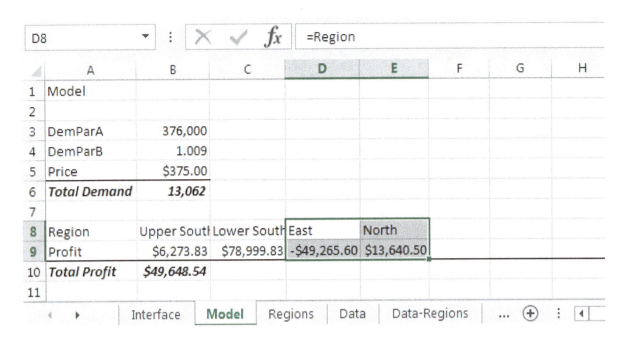

Figure 6-24 Adding a New Region to the Model Sheet

Finally, in the Interface sheet (Figure 6-25), you can now see the profit for all four regions, including the adjusted **Upper South** and **Lower South** regions.

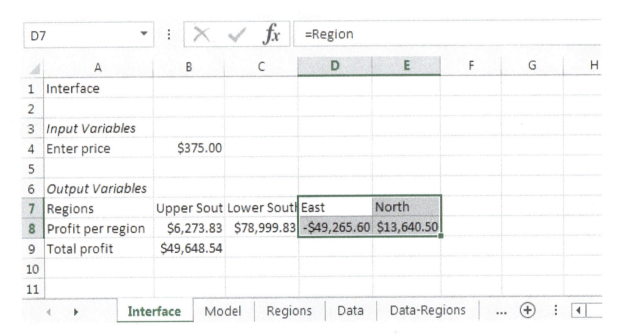

Figure 6-25 Adding a New Region to the Interface Sheet

As you can see, it took you just a few steps to make a major modification to the model—the kind that so often wreaks havoc on poorly structured spreadsheets, causing major inconsistencies. But with this method it's a relatively simple operation, whether it's done by the person who originally built the spreadsheet, or by someone else to whom it was handed off.

Chapter 6 Overview

Here are the main points for you to remember from Chapter 6.

- Implementing a repeating sub-model from the conceptual model is straightforward.
- All variables in the dotted rectangle repeat in the spreadsheet.
- Single-purpose worksheets are used for each repeating entity: one for Data and one for Model.
- Repeating variables are named with the entire-row: select the row number, and name it using the label in _Column A_.
- Use an aggregate function for repeating variables from the sub-model.
- Most importantly, the model is implemented entirely in one column, as one instance of the repeating model; and it's then copied for all the other instances.

Chapter 7 expands the concept of a repeating model by introducing the temporal model.

Chapter 7   Understanding Time in a Spreadsheet

How to use this chapter

This chapter is a leisurely read. But it's not light reading: it explains the temporal reference, which is a key concept that you will use over and over. Allow about 15 minutes.

This chapter presents a special case of the repeating sub-model: the temporal model. When you introduce time periods to a model, you can use their implicit ordering to reference the next period, the previous period, or even two or three periods ago.

Using the Inventory Formula

To understand how to develop a temporal model, you need to use the inventory formula. Businesses use this to calculate their inventory at the end of a certain period (without having to send an employee to physically count the items on the shelves). For the month of January, for instance, the formula can be written as:

Inventory End January = Inventory End December + Purchases During January – Sales During January

This formula is illustrated in Figure 7-1.

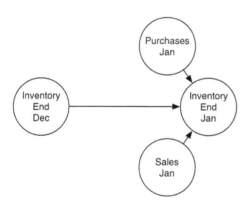

Figure 7-1 Inventory Model, One Month

If you extend this one-month inventory formula over three months, you get the following formulas:

Inventory End Jan = Inventory End Dec + Purchases Jan – Sales Jan

Inventory End Feb = Inventory End Jan + Purchases Feb – Sales Feb

Inventory End Mar = Inventory End Feb + Purchases Mar – Sales Mar

The result of this is shown in Figure 7-2.

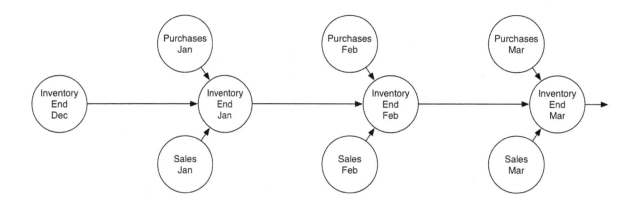

Figure 7-2 Inventory Model, Three Months

This is the same problem you saw when you introduced the repeating sub-model: this structure does not scale well. A 12-month, 24-month or 60-month model would become impractically large and unwieldy. You would like to be able to identify a group of repeating variables and formulas with the same suffix, so that you can build a repeating group (as you did earlier in Chapter 5). However, the formula that calculates the end-of-month inventory uses variables with two different suffixes.

The key to simplifying the model is to create a new calculated variable for each time instance, which acts as an intermediary between one period and the next. Consider the model presented in Figure 7-3.

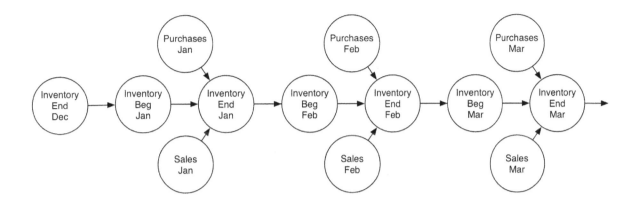

Figure 7-3 Inventory Model With Split Variables

As you can see, introducing a new variable lets you represent the inventory at the beginning of each period. At first this variable may seem redundant, because its value is always equal to the inventory at end of the previous period. However, its value lies in its power to adapt to different circumstances. With this new variable, the formula to calculate the end-of-January inventory now becomes:

Inventory End Jan = Inventory Beg Jan + Purchases Jan – Sales Jan.

Because all the variables in this inventory formula have the same suffix, you can now create a repeating sub-model. These formulas might look like this.

For January:

Inventory Beg Jan = Inventory End Dec

Inventory End Jan = Inventory Beg Jan + Purchases Jan – Sales Jan

For February:

Inventory Beg Feb = Inventory End Jan

Inventory End Feb = Inventory Beg Feb + Purchases Feb – Sales Feb

For March:

Inventory Beg Mar = Inventory End Feb

Inventory End Mar = Inventory Beg Mar + Purchases Mar – Sales Mar

If you examine these formulas closely, you'll notice that they can all be summarized by these two basic formulas:

Inventory Beg (current month) = Inventory End (previous month)

Inventory End = Inventory Beg + Purchases – Sales

A common modelling concept that's useful here is the time reference formula: *(t)*. It's informally referred to as a "corkscrew"—a visual representation of the concept of continuously going either back or forth a certain period of time—and can be used to represent any point relative to the current time: *t-1*, *t+1*, *t-2*, etc. In this case, you can represent the ***previous month*** relationship by using the indicator *(t–1)* next to the arrowhead, as illustrated in Figure 7-4.

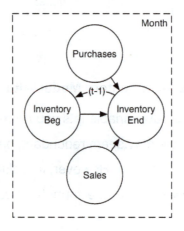

Figure 7-4 Inventory Model in a Repeating Sub-Model

The *(t–1)* arrow indicates that Inventory at the beginning of the period is equal to Inventory at the end of the previous period. An example of this is shown in Figure 7-5, which illustrates how to implement the inventory formula discussed above. Figure 7-5 also illustrates an important fact: when you reference a previous period, you need to supply an initial inventory value. In this case, the almost empty December column is the place to enter that value.

Variable	Dec	Jan	Feb	Mar
Inventory beginning of month		$10,000.00	$9,000.00	$11,000.00
Purchases		$2,000.00	$4,000.00	$2,500.00
Sales		-$3,000.00	-$2,000.00	-$6,400.00
Inventory end of month	*$10,000.00*	*$9,000.00*	*$11,000.00*	*$7,100.00*
Inventory end of month	$10,000.00	$9,000.00	$11,000.00	$7,100.00
Inventory beginning of month		*$10,000.00*	*$9,000.00*	*$11,000.00*

Figure 7-5 A Three-Month Inventory Model

Chapter 7 Overview

Here are the main points for you to remember from Chapter 7.

- The temporal model is similar to the repeating sub-model in its approach of grouping together similar variables and relationships into a repeating structure. What the temporal model adds is the concept of time periods.

- Two important concepts are the beginning and end of a period, where the beginning of the current period is equal to the end of the previous period.

- You were introduced to two new variables, **Inventory End** and **Inventory Beg**, designed to link the time periods.

- Also introduced was the concept of the time reference *(t–1)* to create time relationships between variables.

Chapter 8 will apply these concepts to Marco's situation, allowing you to create a spreadsheet from the conceptual model

Chapter 8   Developing a Temporal Model

How to use this chapter

You should get more involved in this chapter. Take two sheets of paper and draw the Formula Diagram on one and write the Formula List on the other as you read through the chapter. It may seem pointless to do so, but there is a pedagogical value to do it: as you draw the diagram, you will be thinking about what you just read and you will ask yourself questions. I found that students who did that were quicker to understand the modelling steps. Allow about one hour.

Marco's Widgets With Monthly Demand

To illustrate how to develop a temporal model, let's look again at Marco's Widgets. There is a voluntary flaw in the model and it may become apparent when you test it. We will correct it in Chapter 10—thereby demonstrating the basis for the iterative nature of modelling.

To get a better grasp on his monthly widget inventory, Marco needs information on how demand is spread out over the year. He analyzed sales records from previous years, and found that the distribution was as presented in Table 8-1.

Table 8-1 Distribution of *Annual Demand*

Jan	Feb	Mar	Apr	May	June	July	Aug	Sept	Oct	Nov	Dec
8%	9%	10%	15%	11%	7%	5%	10%	6%	5%	6%	8%

As well as the distribution of demand, Marco wants to add another improvement to his model. His first version did not consider monthly inventory separately, so he included the cost of the inventory in the data variable **Unit Cost**. But now that he can calculate his monthly inventory, he wants the model to track its cost as well. To do this, he splits the former **Unit Cost** into two variables:

- inventory cost (**Unit Inventory Cost = $20**)
- the cost of producing and selling the widgets (**Unit Sales Cost = $150**).

The **Unit Inventory Cost** will be used with the inventory at the end of each month and the **Unit Sales Cost** will be used with the monthly **Demand**.

At the moment, Marco's machines are set to produce 1,200 widgets per month. Resetting the machines to produce at a different rate is a complicated operation, one that can only be done once a year. Marco wants to use the model to evaluate the impact on his profit of different monthly production-rate scenarios. The next section will examine this process.

Temporal Formula Diagram

To start developing a temporal model, draw a dotted-line rectangle in your Formula Diagram to represent the repeating sub-model. Inside it, insert your repeating variables (all those with a value corresponding to its instance in time); and around it, place the single-value variables. Figure 8-1 shows such a model, using the variables from Chapter 5 and Chapter 7.

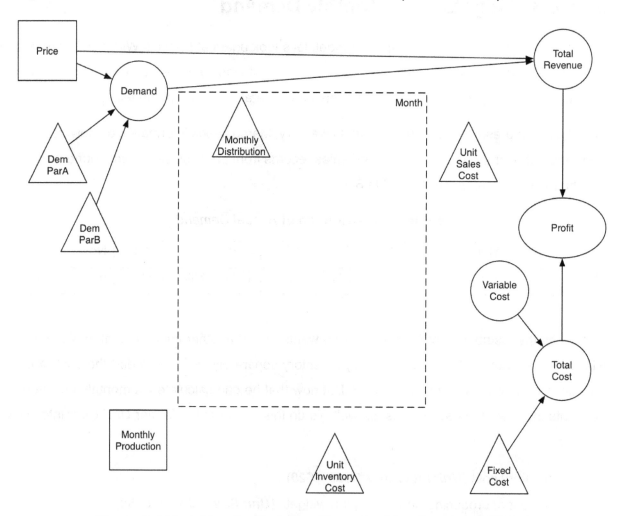

Figure 8-1 Variables Carried Over From the Non-Temporal Model

In this diagram, notice that **Monthly Production** is outside the repeating sub-model. Despite its name, this is not in fact a monthly variable—that would be one that represents 12 values, like **Monthly Distribution**. Since **Monthly Production** represents a single value (1,200 widgets at present), it's not a temporal variable. "Monthly," in this case, refers to the fact that the machines are set at a specific monthly production rate, but the rate is fixed for the year.

Now it's time to again update the Formula List, and add the five new items that involve the temporal model: **Variable Cost**, **Monthly Distribution**, **Monthly Production**, **Unit Sales Cost**, and **Unit Inventory Cost**. These variables are described in Table 8-2.

Table 8-2 Temporal Model

Variable	Type	Definition
Price	Input	*(To be set by user)*
DemParA	Data	*376,000*
DemParB	Data	*1.009*
Fixed Cost	Data	*$2,500,000*
Demand	Calculated	*DemParA * DemParB^-Price*
Total Cost	Calculated	*Fixed Cost + Variable Cost*
Total Revenue	Calculated	*Demand * Price*
Variable Cost	Calculated	*?*
Monthly Distribution	Data, Month	*Set of 12 values*
Monthly Production	Input	*(To be set by user)*
Unit Sales Cost	Data	*$150*
Unit Inventory Cost	Data	*$20*

Now continue building the model, using either the forward or the backward approach. With the former, from **Demand** and **Monthly Distribution** you can calculate the formula as shown below.

Variable	Type	Definition
Monthly Demand	Calculated, Month	*Demand * Monthly Distribution*

Since this new variable is calculated using a temporal variable, it's in itself a temporal variable; so you should put it inside the temporal sub-model rectangle, as shown in Figure 8-2.

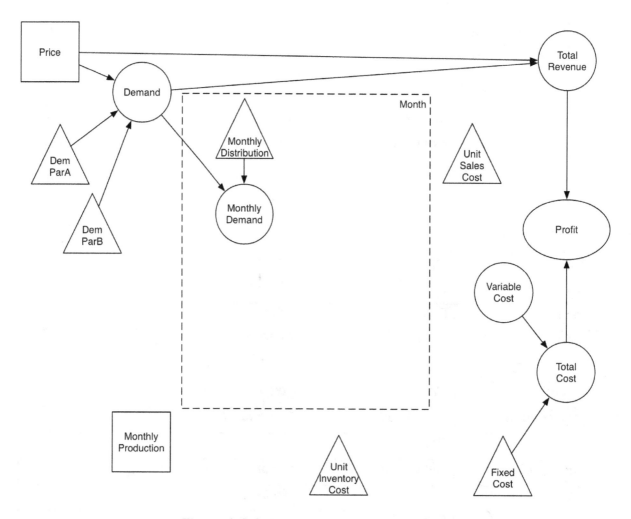

Figure 8-2 Calculating Monthly Demand

You now have all the elements you need to calculate the variables and formulas of the inventory formula. ***Monthly Demand*** represents sales (output), and ***Monthly Production*** represents purchases (input). The two new formulas to calculate the inventory are shown below.

Variable	Type	Definition
Inventory End	Calculated, Month	***Inventory Beg + Monthly Production – Monthly Demand; Initial Inventory = 1500***
Inventory Beg	Calculated, Month	***Inventory End (t–1)***

The initial value of a variable involved in a time reference formula, ***Inventory End*** in this case, is specified in its definition formula. This will ensure that the first column of the model's implementation is the same as all the others.

The initial value is implicit, and we don't need to show it in the Formula Diagram, as illustrated in Figure 8-3.

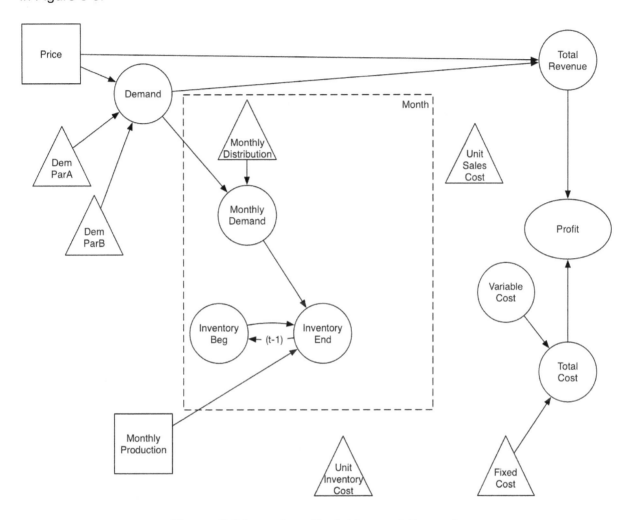

Figure 8-3 Inventory Variables and Formula

This allows you to calculate the monthly *Inventory Cost* and the monthly *Sales Cost* as shown below.

Variable	Type	Definition
Inventory Cost	Calculated, Month	*Inventory End * Unit Inventory Cost*
Sales Cost	Calculated, Month	*Monthly Demand * Unit Sales Cost*

These two new variables are shown in Figure 8-4.

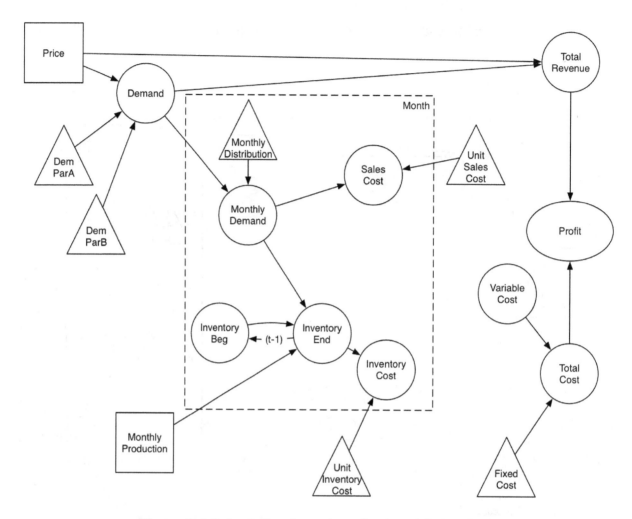

Figure 8-4 Calculating Inventory Cost and Sales Cost

You now have two variables with no outgoing arrows, and one variable with no incoming arrow. You might be tempted to define this formula:

Variable Cost = SUM(Sales Cost) + SUM(Inventory Cost).

But that would go against the Simplicity Rule, which forbids a formula from mixing different operators. (You might argue that the operator **+** and the function **_SUM_** are the same, but they are not: a function, no matter what it is, should be a formula by itself.) This leaves you with two equivalent possibilities, illustrated below. The first option uses the following formulas.

Variable	Type	Definition
Monthly Variable Cost	Calculated, Month	**_Inventory Cost + Sales Cost_**
Variable Cost	Calculated	**_SUM(Monthly Variable Cost)_**

The result of this is shown in Figure 8-5.

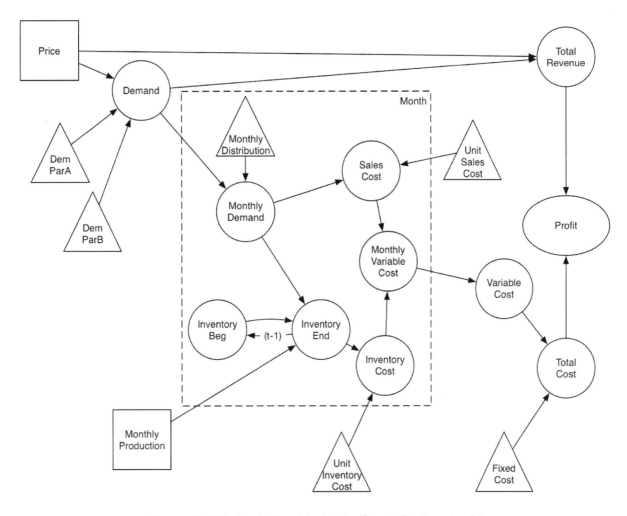

Figure 8-5 Calculating Variable Cost, Option 1 of 2

The second option uses the following formulas.

Variable	Type	Definition
Total Sales Cost	Calculated	*SUM(Sales Cost)*
Total Inventory Cost	Calculated	*SUM(Inventory Cost)*
Variable Cost	Calculated	*Total Sales Cost + Total Inventory Cost*

We see this second option of calculating *Variable Cost* in Figure 8-6.

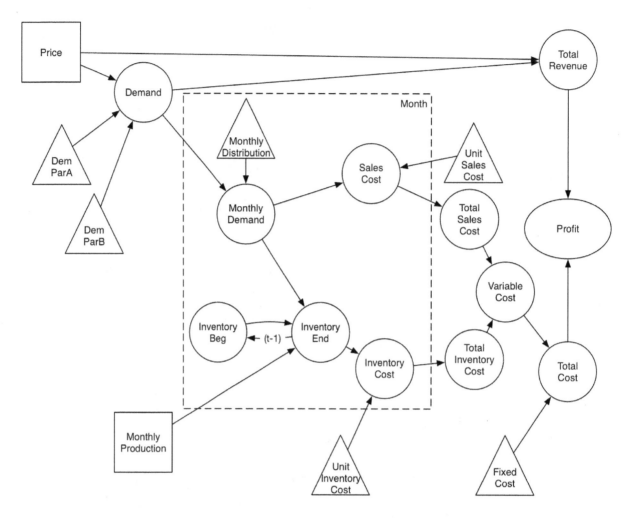

Figure 8-6 Calculating Variable Cost, Option 2 of 2

Mathematically, both models are equivalent. As their builder, you decide where you prefer to have more detail. You can either calculate the variable cost as an aggregate function (Figure 8-5), or calculate it entirely outside of the rectangle (Figure 8-6, above).

In the next chapter, you'll implement the former, as shown in Figure 8-5. Its formula list is presented in Table 8-3.

Table 8-3 Formula List, Temporal Model

Variable	Type	Definition
Price	Input	*(To be set by user)*
Profit	Output	*Total Revenue – Total Cost*
DemParA	Data	*376,000*
DemParB	Data	*1.009*
Fixed Cost	Data	*$2,500,000*

Variable	Type	Definition
Annual Demand	Calculated	**DemParA * DemParB^-Price**
Total Cost	Calculated	**Fixed Cost + Total Variable Cost**
Variable Cost	Calculated	**Sum(Monthly Variable Cost)**
Total Revenue	Calculated	**Annual Demand * Price**
Monthly Distribution	Data, Month	**Set of 12 values**
Monthly Production	Input	**(To be set by user)**
Unit Sales Cost	Data	**$150**
Unit Inventory Cost	Data	**$20**
Monthly Demand	Calculated, Month	**Annual Demand * Monthly Distribution**
Inventory End	Calculated, Month	**Inventory Beg + Monthly Production – Monthly Demand; Initial Inventory = 1500**
Inventory Beg	Calculated, Month	**Inventory End(t–1)**
Inventory Cost	Calculated, Month	**Inventory End * Unit Inventory Cost**
Sales Cost	Calculated, Month	**Monthly Demand * Unit Sales Cost**
Monthly Variable Cost	Calculated, Month	**Inventory Cost + Sales Cost**

Chapter 8 Overview

Here are the main points for you to remember from Chapter 8.

- Presenting time as a repeating entity makes it simpler for you to conceptualize.
- Using beginning and end variables lets you link two instances.
- When these variables are joined by a time reference *(t–1)*, the value at the beginning of the current period is always the same as the value at the end of the previous period.

Chapter 9 will tackle the next phase: implementing the temporal model into a spreadsheet.

Chapter 9   Implementing a Temporal Model

How to use this chapter

As in the previous chapter, you should reproduce the spreadsheet implementation as you read through the whole chapter. I suggest that you put a check mark next to the variables on the Formula Diagram and the Formula List as you implement them. Pay attention to the way we go back and forth between the different worksheets. Allow about one hour.

The last chapter examined two equivalent models, which differed only in the way they calculated Variable Cost. This chapter will look at how to create a temporal model from the following structured conceptual model, shown in Figure 9-1.

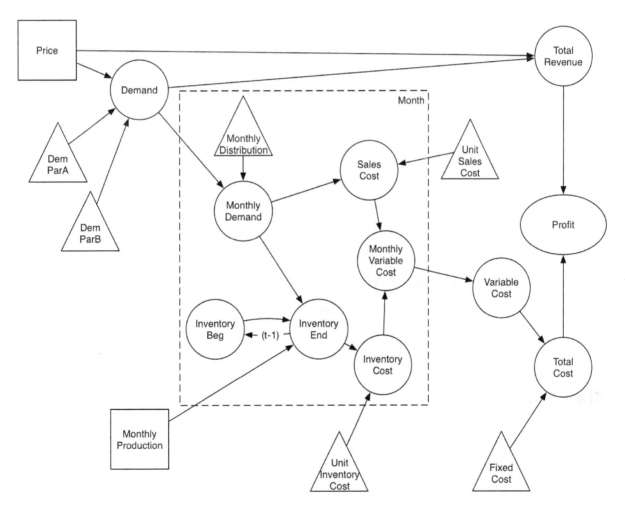

Figure 9-1 Temporal Model

The steps required to create a temporal model are similar to those of a repeating sub-model, but with some new elements. One difference is the need for an initialization period (in this case, previous period) to implement the temporal reference.

Implementing a Three-Tier Architecture

As in Chapter 6, create a three-tier architecture with five sheets:

- one data sheet contains the non-repeating data variables (**Data**),
- another data sheet contains the repeating data variables (**Data-Months**),
- one model sheet contains the definition formulas of all the non-temporal calculated variables (**Model**),
- another model sheet contains the definition formulas of all the temporal variables, with the repeating instances of the periods (**Months**),
- the **Interface** sheet contains all the inputs and outputs you need to manipulate.

These five sheets are all illustrated in Figure 9-2.

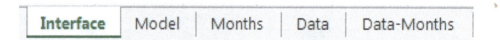

Figure 9-2 Sheet Names of the Temporal Three-Tier Architecture

The three steps to designing this temporal model are:

- Step 1: Entering the Data Variables
- Step 2: Defining the Calculated Variables
- Step 3: Formatting the **Interface** Sheet

These steps are defined in the following sections.

Step 1: Entering the Data Variables

This step involves creating two data sheets, one for non-repeating data variables (**Data**, Step 1.1), and one for repeating data variables (**Data-Months**, Step 1.2).

Step 1.1: Non-Repeating Data Variables

Start by entering variables into the **Data** sheet, starting with the single-value data variables names in *Column A*. Then enter their corresponding values into *Column B*, as shown in Figure 9-3.

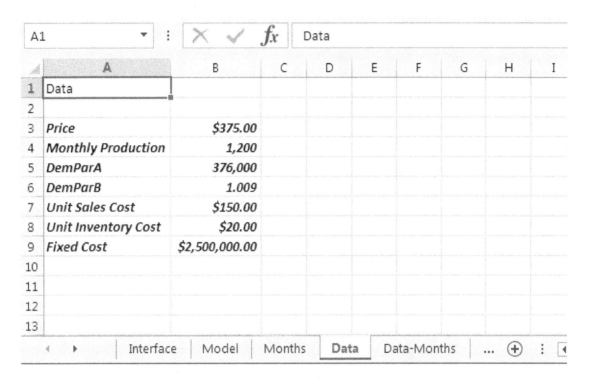

Figure 9-3 Step 1.1, Entering Single-Value Data Variables

Then name the single-value data variables, using the labels in *Column A*, as illustrated in Figure 9-4.

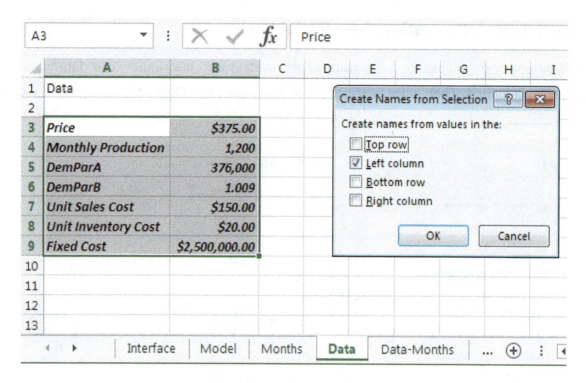

Figure 9-4 Step 1.1, Naming Single-Value Data Variables

Step 1.2: Repeating Data Variables

Now specify the repeating variables in the **Data-Months** sheet—but first you need to specify the initial values of all the variables used in a *(t–1)* reference, and name the values accordingly. In this case, *Initial Inventory* is the only initial value, as shown in Figure 9-5. (Note that the initial values do not appear in the Formula Diagram, but they are specified in the Formula List, like when we wrote the formula for *Inventory End*.)

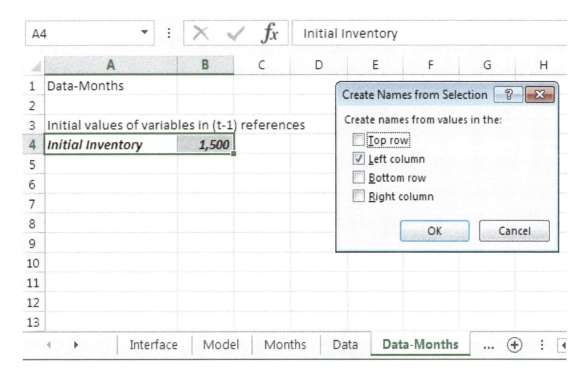

Figure 9-5 Step 1.2, Naming the Initial Values of Multi-Value Data Variables

Now define the repeating entity and the multi-value data variables. In this case the repeating entity is **Month**, so enter it and the multi-value data variable names into *Column A*. Next enter the name of the instances, alongside the entity name, beginning with the previous month (to let you model the *(t–1)* references properly). Since this model starts in January, the first name in *Column B* is December, as shown in Figure 9-6.

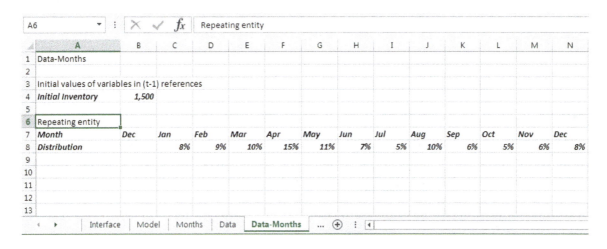

Figure 9-6 Step 1.2, Defining the Repeating Entity and its Data Variables

Finally, name the entity and the multiple-value data variables. Select the entire rows (by clicking on the *Row Number* on the left side). Then use the *Create Names From Selection* dialogue box and make sure that *Left column* is the only checkbox selected, as shown in Figure 9-7.

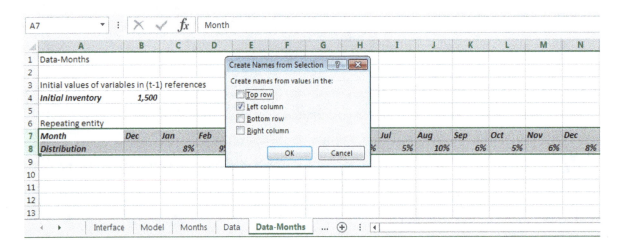

Figure 9-7 Step 1.2, Naming the Repeating Entity and its Data Variables

When dealing with data variables that represent a distribution, you can verify their correctness by checking that their sum is 100%. For that purpose, you may want to insert a validation formula below the data variable to check its sum, as shown in Figure 9-8. (Validation formulas are presented in more detail in Chapter 12.)

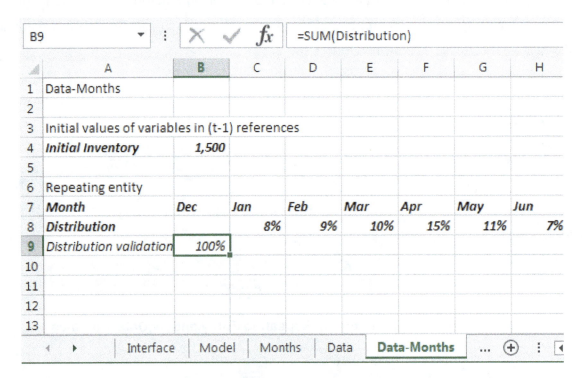

Figure 9-8 Step 1.2, Validating a Multi-Value Data Variable

Step 2: Defining the Calculated Variables

This step involves creating two model sheets: one for the definition formulas of all non-temporal calculated variables (**Model**, Step 2.1), and the other for the definition formulas of all the temporal variables (**Months**, Step 2.2).

All your calculated variables must have their formulas defined in either the **Model** or the **Months** sheet. From previous chapters, you know how to set up the **Model** sheet. But the **Months** sheet is slightly different. While it resembles the repeating sub-model sheet from Chapter 5, it needs a few extra operations to correctly represent the *(t–1)* references.

Step 2.1: The Model Sheet

Start by entering the definition formulas of your calculated variables that are defined only by variables outside the repeating temporal model. Here you have two, as shown in Figure 9-9: *Annual Demand* and *Total Revenue*.

	Total_Revenue	▼ :	✕ ✓ ƒx	=B8*B9			
◢	A		B	C	D	E	F
1	Model						
2							
3	DemParA		376,000				
4	DemParB		1.009				
5	Price		$375.00				
6	*Annual Demand*		*13,062*				
7							
8	Annual Demand		13,062				
9	Price		$375.00				
10	*Total Revenue*		*$4,898,146.54*				
11							
12							
13							

| ◂ ▸ | Interface | **Model** | Months | Data | Data-Months | ... ⊕ : ◂ |

Figure 9-9 Step 2.1, Starting the Model Sheet

However, some calculated variables—such as *Total Cost* and *Profit*–can't yet be implemented. Even though their definition formulas use only variables from outside the repeating sub-model, they depend on *Variable Cost*, which itself depends on a repeating variable. You must wait until the **Months** sheet is completed to enter the formulas for these variables. After Step 2.2 you'll see that Step 2.1 is continued a few pages hence.

Step 2.2: The Temporal Model Sheet

In this model, the repeating model sheet will be **Months**. To develop the **Months** sheet, start with the initialization periods and the first period of the model. Here you have only one initialization period, December, and the model starts with January. Enter the label of the repeating entity **Month** in _Column A_, and its reference formula, **=Month**, in _Column B_. Then copy the formula into _Column C_, as illustrated in Figure 9-10.

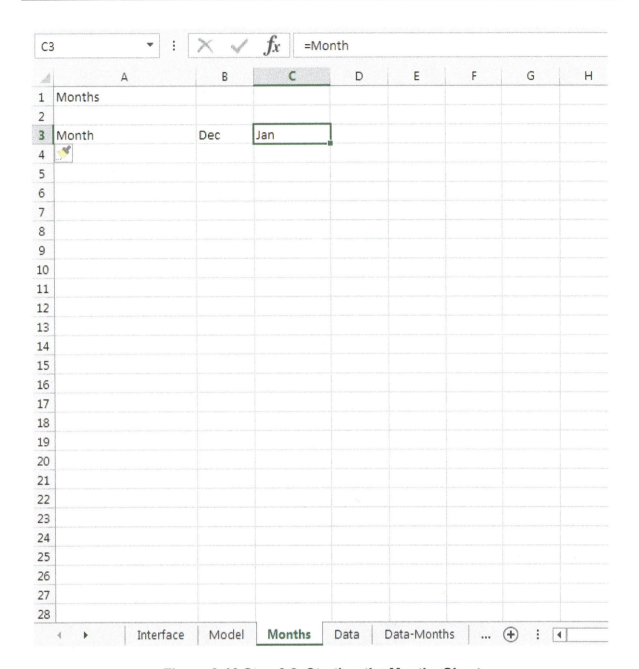

Figure 9-10 Step 2.2, Starting the Months Sheet

Now you can enter the definition formulas for the variables inside the sub-model. Figure 9-11 shows the first block. If you look at _Column C_, you'll notice that it represents the first period, not _Column B_. This is because the variable with a **(t–1)** reference needs an initialization column. (Models with a **(t–2)** reference require two initialization columns, and the model would start in _Column D_.)

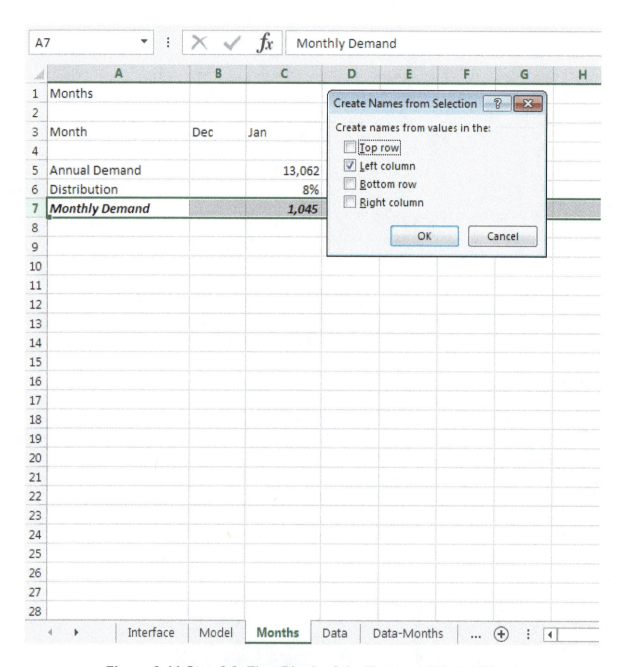

Figure 9-11 Step 2.2, First Block of the Temporal Model Sheet

If you try to define the formula to calculate *Inventory End*, you'll notice a problem: you've already defined *Monthly Production* and *Monthly Demand*, but not *Inventory Beg*. First enter the labels in Column A, then the reference formulas *=Monthly_Prod* in *Cell C10* and *=-Demand* in *Cell C11* (note the minus sign.) Note that you can't enter the reference formula for *Inventory Beg* until you create its definition formula—which you can only do after finishing this block. However, you can enter the full *Inventory End* formula in *Cell C12*, as illustrated in Figure 9-12.

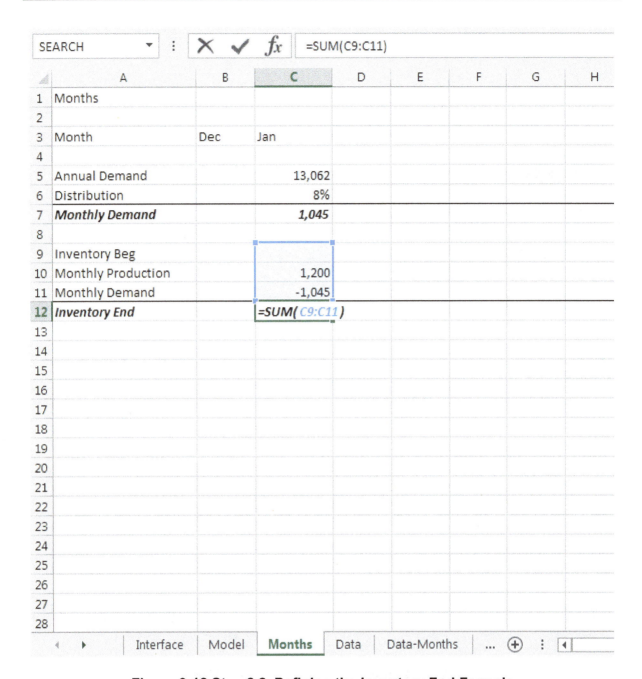

Figure 9-12 Step 2.2, Defining the Inventory End Formula

Because you used a sign-changing reference formula for ***Monthly Demand***, the previous figure used the ***SUM*** function (which includes *Cell C9*, currently empty). Since this is the block where ***Inventory End*** is defined, and since this variable is part of a ***(t–1)*** reference, enter the initialization reference in *Column B*—as shown in Figure 9-13.

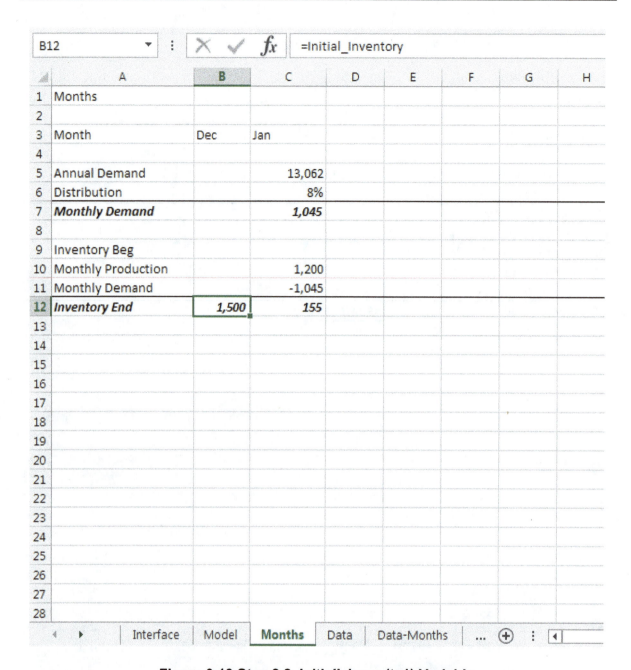

Figure 9-13 Step 2.2, Initializing a (t–1) Variable

Now you can finally enter and name the definition of **Inventory Beg**. Since it depends only on **Inventory End**, enter the labels in *Column A*, and the reference formula **=Inventory_End** in *Column C*. But since this is a *(t–1)* reference, you also need to enter the formula in *Column B*. This is shown in Figure 9-14.

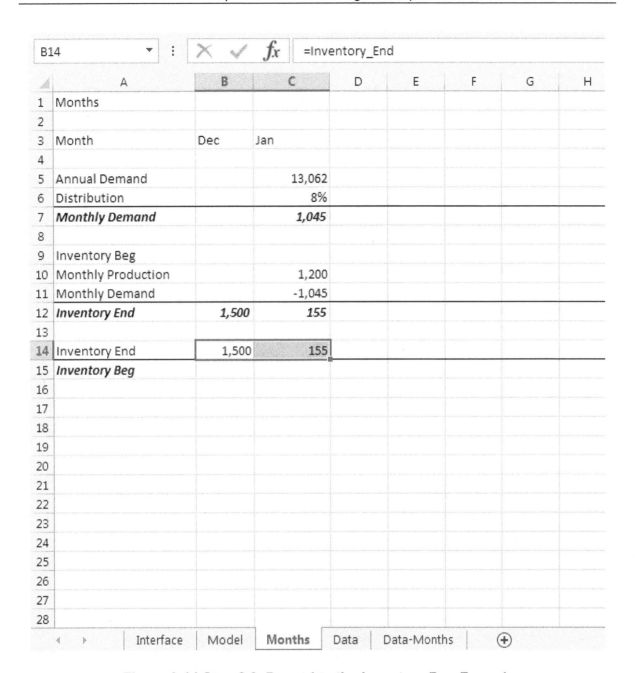

Figure 9-14 Step 2.2, Preparing the Inventory Beg Formula

Finally, define **Inventory Beg** by referring to **Inventory End** of the previous period, namely **=B14**. To finish, select _Row 15_ to apply the top border and create the name, as illustrated in Figure 9-15.

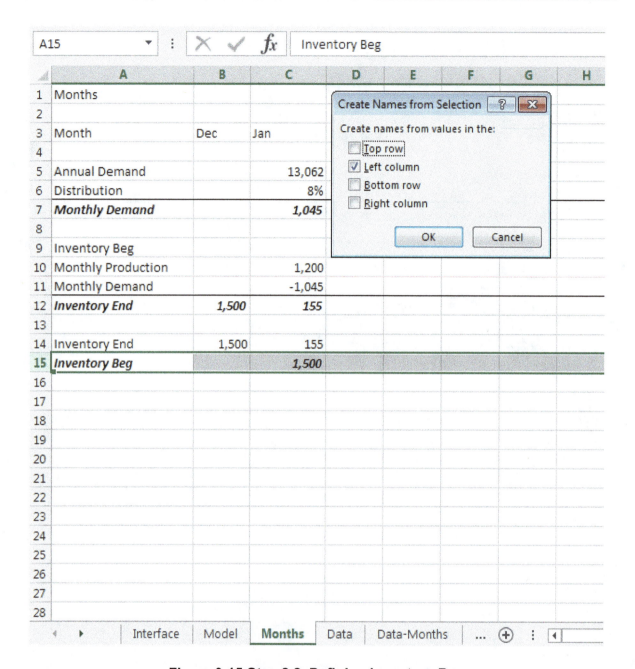

Figure 9-15 Step 2.2, Defining Inventory Beg

Now that **Inventory Beg** has been defined, you can complete the **Inventory End** block. In _Cell C9_, you need only write the reference formula **=Inventory_Beg**.

This completes the **Inventory End** block, shown in Figure 9-16.

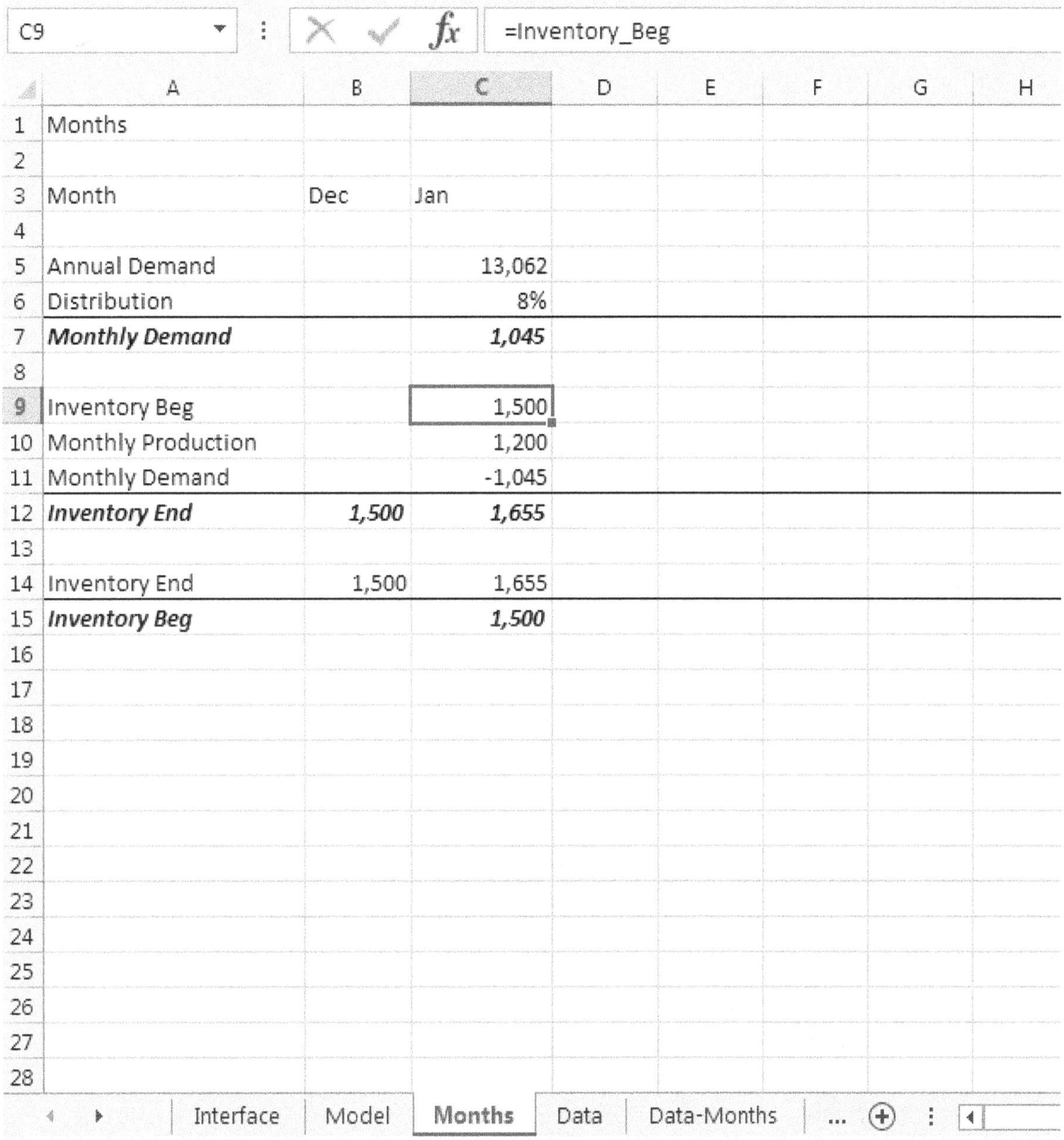

	A	B	C	D	E	F	G	H
	C9	▼ : ✕ ✓ *fx*	=Inventory_Beg					
1	Months							
2								
3	Month	Dec	Jan					
4								
5	Annual Demand		13,062					
6	Distribution		8%					
7	*Monthly Demand*		*1,045*					
8								
9	Inventory Beg		1,500					
10	Monthly Production		1,200					
11	Monthly Demand		-1,045					
12	*Inventory End*	*1,500*	*1,655*					
13								
14	Inventory End	1,500	1,655					
15	*Inventory Beg*		*1,500*					
16								
17								
18								
19								
20								
21								
22								
23								
24								
25								
26								
27								
28								

Interface | Model | **Months** | Data | Data-Months | ... ⊕ ⋮ ◄

Figure 9-16 Step 2.2, Finishing the Inventory End Block

You can define the remaining variables by following the same operations as for ***Demand***, as illustrated in Figure 9-17.

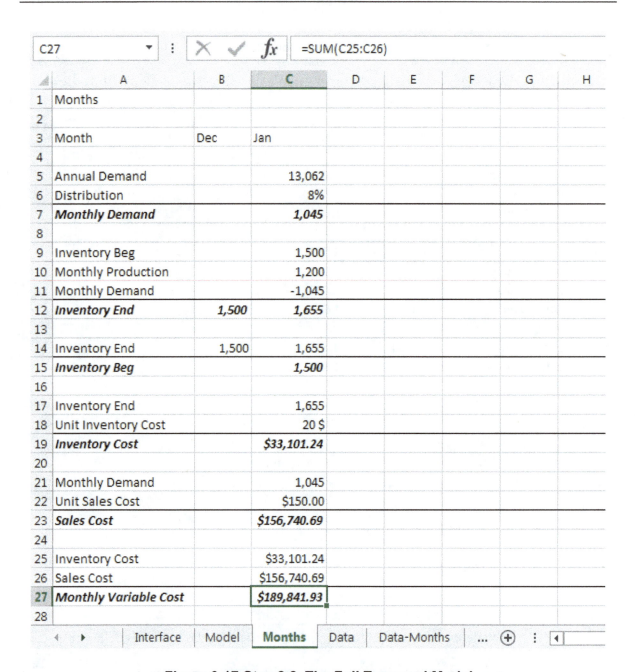

Figure 9-17 Step 2.2, The Full Temporal Model

As shown in Figure 9-18, the model in _Column C_ follows basic implementation guidelines.

- Every variable is defined at the bottom of a block.

- All the variables used to define it are above, and use reference formulas with names.

- There are no superfluous variables (ones not used in the definition formulas).

- Rather than names, all definition formulas use references to cells.

- Except for the **_Inventory Beg_** formula in _Row 15_, which refers to _Column B_, the formulas always refer to _Column C_.

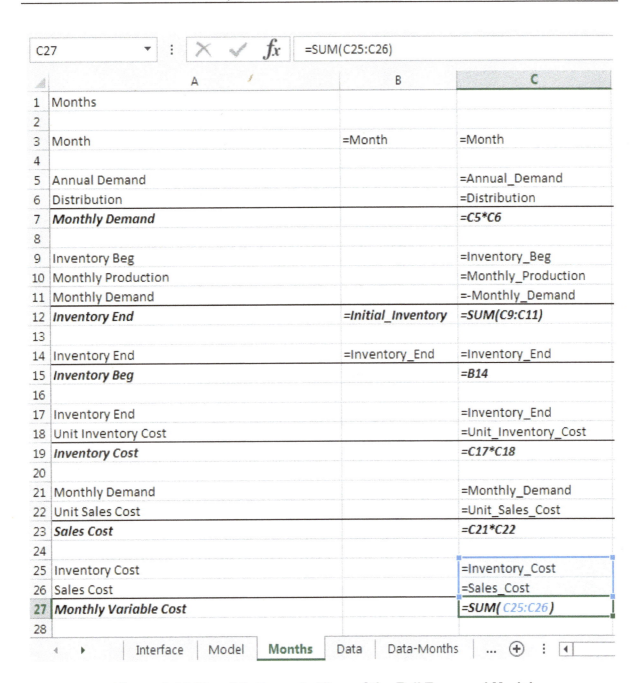

Figure 9-18 Step 2.2, Formula View of the Full Temporal Model

Now that the January model is finished, the last operation you need to perform is to copy all the formulas to the 11 columns on the right, to create a 12-month model. Select the entire *Column C*, and drag the *copy handle* all the way over to *Column N*. Figure 9-19 shows the result.

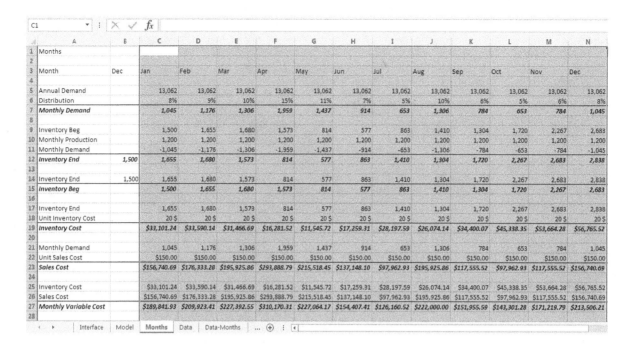

Figure 9-19 Step 2.2, The 12-Month Model

Step 2.1 (Continued): The Finished Model Sheet

As indicated at the end of Step 2.1: The Model Sheet, you still have three variables left to define: **Variable Cost**, **Total Cost** and **Profit**. To calculate the first, you need to handle it in a specific way. As you can see in Figure 9-20 (which shows only a portion of the Formula Diagram), this variable is defined by the arrow leaving the repeating sub-model.

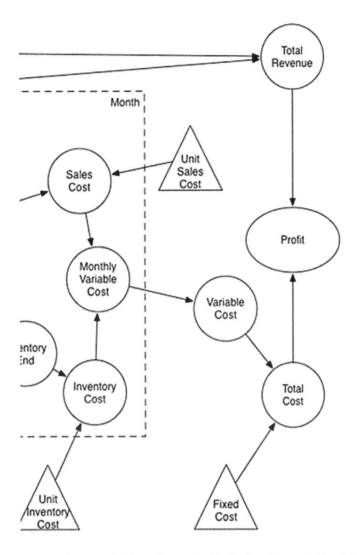

Figure 9-20 Step 2.1 (Continued), Defining Result Variables

You first enter the labels of the variables in _Column A_, along with the sub-model's entity for clarity. This is illustrated in Figure 9-21.

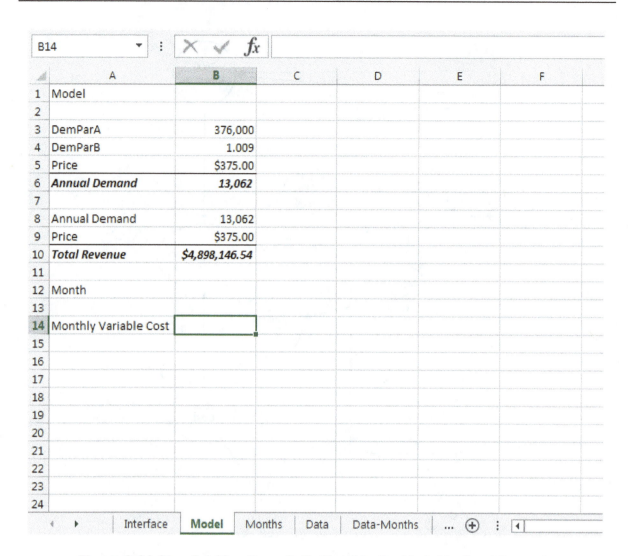

Figure 9-21 Step 2.1 (Continued), Setting Up the Variable Cost Formula

Starting in *Column C*—which corresponds to the first period in the **Month** sheet—enter the reference formula for the repeating entity, **=Month**, and the reference to the variable, **=Monthly_Variable_Cost**. Then copy the formulas to cover all the periods, as shown in Figure 9-22.

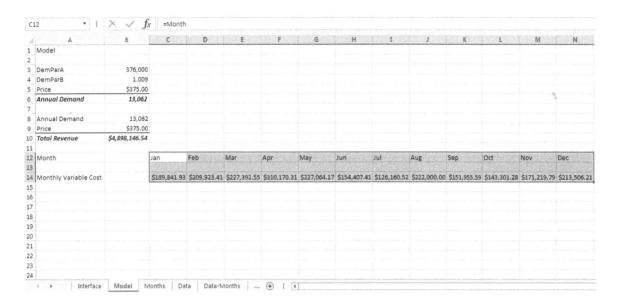

Figure 9-22 Step 2.1 (Continued), Reference Formulas for all Periods

Finally, enter the definition formula of *Variable Cost* and name it, as illustrated in Figure 9-23.

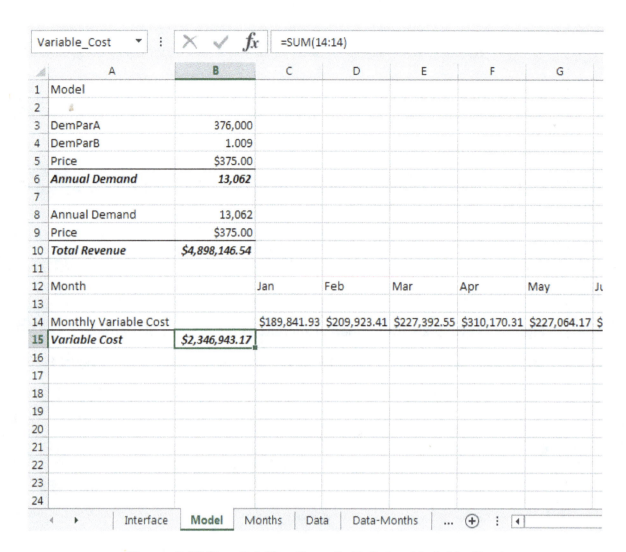

Figure 9-23 Step 2.1 (Continued), Defining Variable Cost

After you've done this, writing the definition and naming the two remaining variables is straightforward. The result in shown in Figure 9-24.

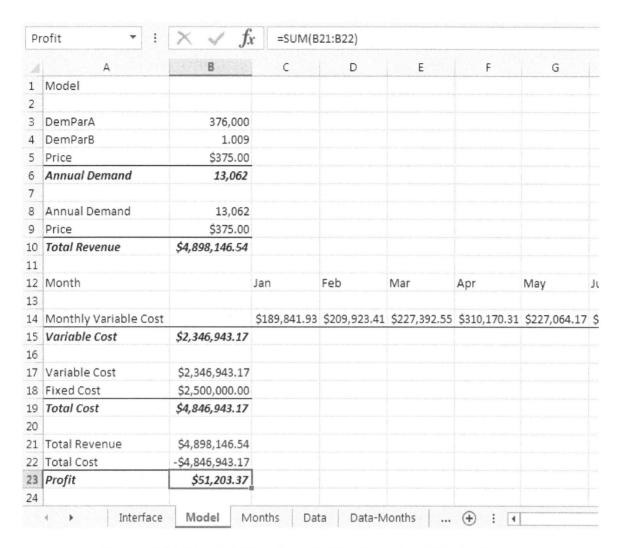

Figure 9-24 Step 2.1 (Continued), The Completed Model Sheet

The formula view of the completed **Model** sheet is shown in Figure 9-25.

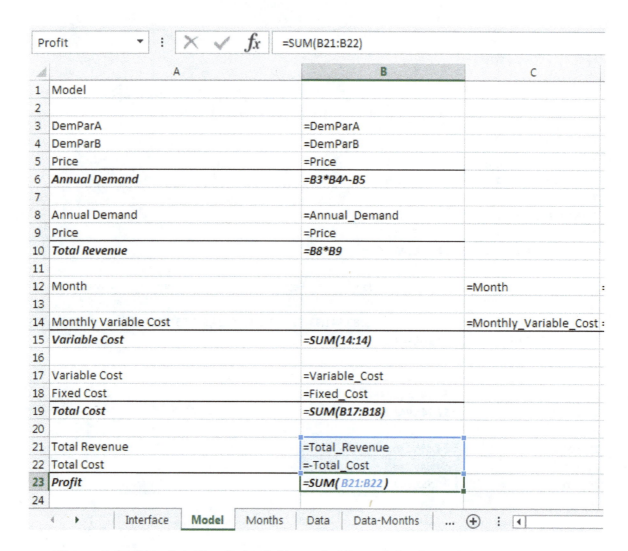

Figure 9-25 Step 2.1 (Continued), Formula View of the Completed Model Sheet

Step 3: Implementing the Interface Sheet

The final step consists of implementing the **Interface** sheet. This sheet will hold the input variables, defined in the **Data** sheet. In Figure 9-26 you can see that the two input variables are entered as constants.

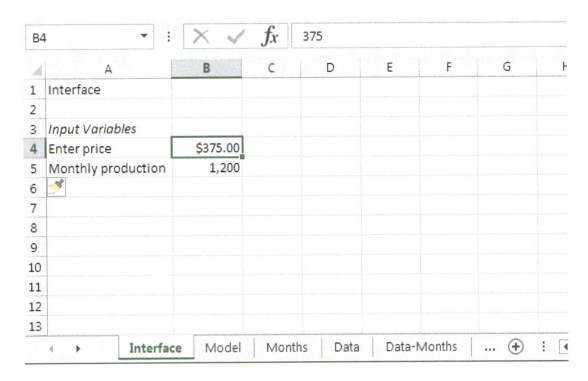

Figure 9-26 Step 3, Input Variables in the Interface Sheet

Again, when you enter input values to the **Interface** sheet, it's important that you reference these cells properly in the **Data** sheet—as shown in Figure 9-27.

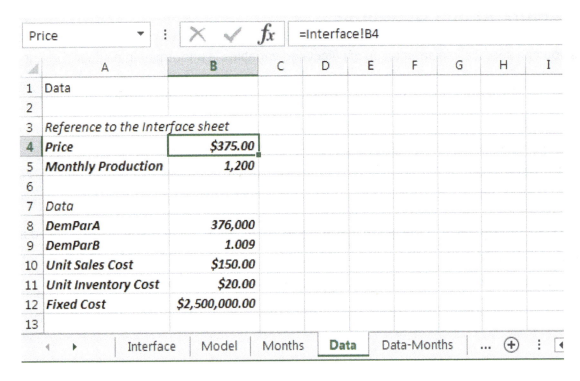

Figure 9-27 Step 3, Input Variables in the Data Sheet

Finally, enter the output variable references in the **Interface** sheet, as shown in Figure 9-28.

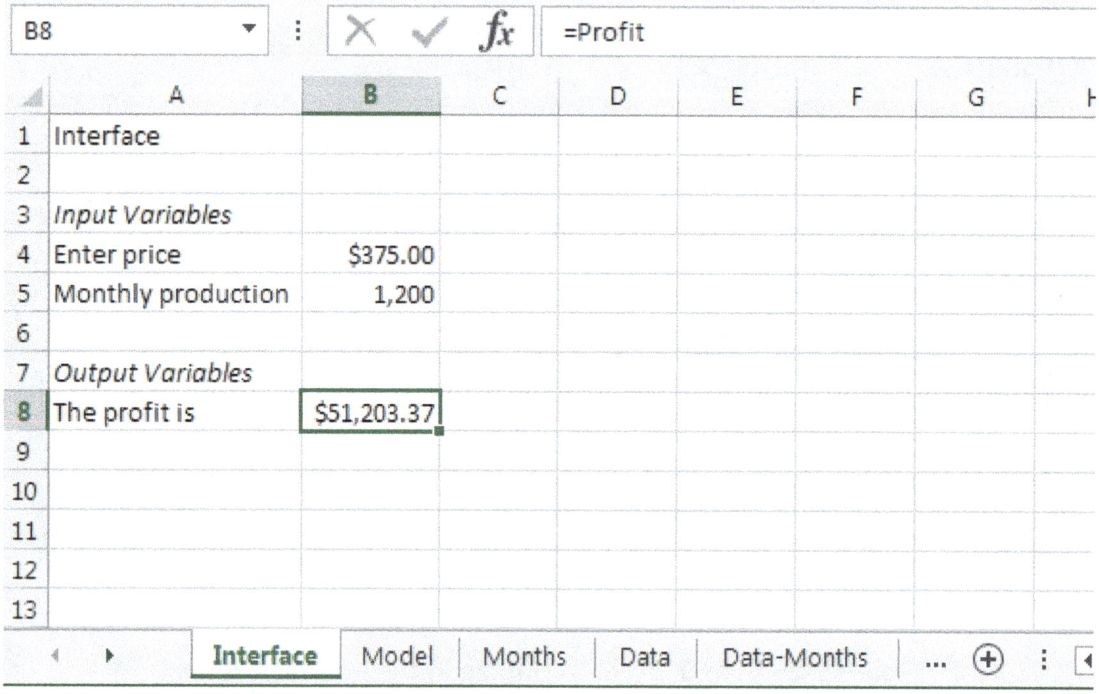

Figure 9-28 Step 3, Output Variables in the Interface Sheet

Implementation Sequence

As you can see, the implementation of calculated variables is performed in a specific sequence:

- in the **Model** sheet you enter variables that don't depend (directly or indirectly) on repeating variables;
- you develop the **Months** sheet to define all repeating variables;
- you go back to the **Model** sheet to implement the variables that depend on repeating variables.

This standard sequence is one you'll use many times in creating spreadsheets—and if you need to create complex models, the process may require even more iterations. You may find that you need to alternate a few times between the **Model** and **Repeating Model** sheets.

Chapter 9 Overview

Here are the main points for you to remember from Chapter 9.

- The repeating entity is always a time factor: days, years, months, periods, etc.
- The period-end variable and the period-beginning variable are both implemented in their own separate blocks.
- Use an initial value in the initialization period to define the period-end variable.
- Use the period-beginning variable in the definition formula of the period-end variable.

Chapter 10, up next, discusses how to modify and maintain a model.

Part II Overview

The tools you've learned to use in Part II give you the technical basis to solve a variety of spreadsheet problems. Using repeating sub-models and/or temporal models, the combination of structure and flexibility allows you to build models as diverse as a financial forecasting spreadsheet, a spreadsheet to keep track of your Air Miles points, a project-management spreadsheet, or any other decision-support system that can be built in a spreadsheet.

- Here are some points for you to keep in mind when developing such models.
- Always begin by conceptualizing your model.
- Build your Formula Diagram and Formula List. (You don't even need to open Excel until you've thought through the problem!)
- Separate all your variables into types. What are your outputs? What are your inputs? What are your data variables? What are your calculated variables?
- Keep your formulas simple—only one mathematical operator in each.
- Identify when you need to use a repeating sub-model. Years and regions are common repeating entities, though others might be more useful for your specific needs.
- Separate the implementation into three types of single-purpose worksheets: the data sheets (non-repeating and repeating), the model sheets (non-repeating and repeating), and the **Interface** sheet.
- Name single-value variables, and use an entire row to name multiple-value variables.
- Use the block structure to define calculated variables. Use name references for all the variables above the line (those that define a calculated variable), and use a reference for those cells in the formula that are below the line.
- Use aggregate functions to calculate variables that result from the repeating sub-model.
- Use the **Interface** sheet to present all the information users might need to manipulate. Reference these values from the data sheet(s), and use name references to present the outputs.

Part III of this book, in the chapters that follow, looks at some more in-depth concepts: how to modify an existing model, explore different modelling techniques, and maintain spreadsheets.

Part III: Learning Advanced SSMI Topics

Chapter 10: Modifying a Model

- Modifying the Formula Diagram
- Modifying the Spreadsheet

Chapter 11: Using Advanced Modelling Techniques

- Modelling Special Cases
- Example: Using State Indicator Variables
- Looking Forward in Time

Chapter 12: Managing Spreadsheets

- Checking for Errors
- Using Model Management Formulas
- Protecting Worksheets

Chapter 10   Modifying a Model

How to use this chapter

Take the Formula Diagram and the Formula List you prepared when you worked on Chapter 8. This chapter leads you through the steps of modifying a model and its implementation. It's a normal process: you will always have to modify a model to improve it or to correct errors. Allow about one hour.

In some situations, you may need to modify a model—either after it has been built, if you discover some flaws during testing; or later in its lifecycle, if you decide to reconfigure it to meet new requirements. Such corrections and enhancements to satisfy changing needs are called maintenance.

To illustrate the steps of a maintenance operation, consider Marco's Widgets. In Chapter 8, you may have noticed an important flaw: the model assumed that Marco's monthly production level would always allow him to satisfy demand. In practice, Marco could possibly produce less than the demand.

Let's re-examine that final model from Figure 8-5. It's shown again in Figure 10-1.

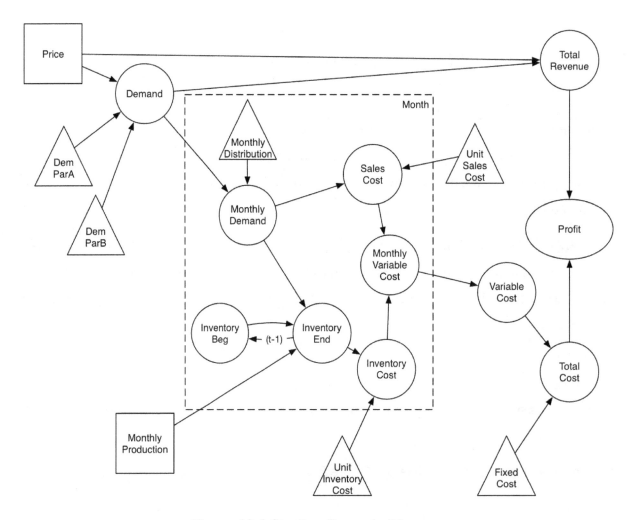

Figure 10-1 Starting Formula Diagram

Modifying the Formula Diagram

To model the fact that the number of widgets sold may not necessarily match the demand, you introduce a new intermediate variable: Sales. This represents the quantity sold each month, as illustrated (in grey) in Figure 10-2.

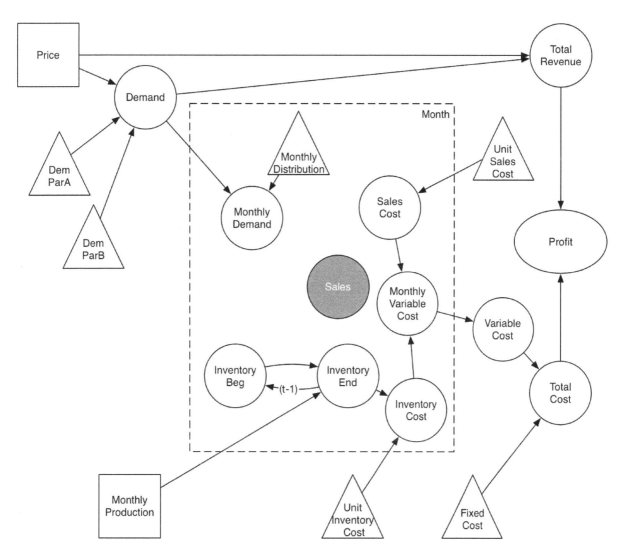

Figure 10-2 Adding Sales

You now need to find out which other formulas are affected by the introduction of **Sales**. One obvious example is **Sales Cost**, and another formula is **Inventory End**. These two formulas are calculated as shown below.

Variable	Type	Definition
Sales Cost	Calculated, Month	**Sales * Unit Sales Cost**
Inventory End	Calculated, Month	**Inventory Beg + Monthly Prod – Sales**

Another formula is **Inventory End**, which should now be calculated as:

Inventory End = Inventory Beg + Monthly Prod – Sales.

These changes are shown (in grey), in Figure 10-3.

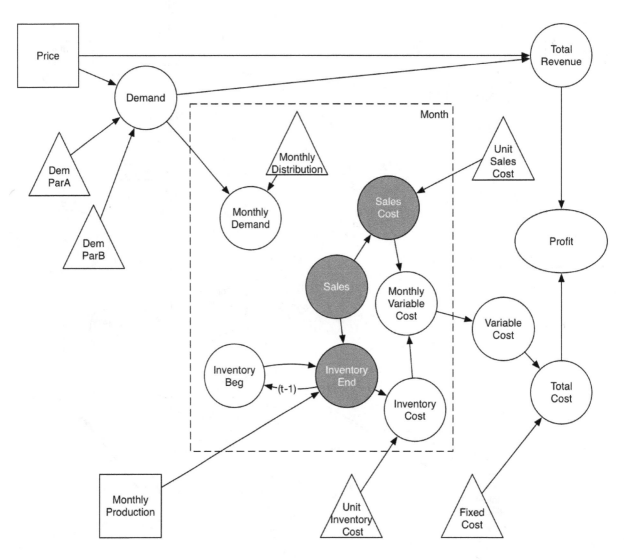

Figure 10-3 Influence of Sales on Sales Cost and Inventory End

You should also use the new **Sales** variable to calculate **Total Revenue**. In the original calculation, **Demand** was outside the temporal model—since it was assumed that Mario would sell all his supply. But now you can calculate **Monthly Revenue** as a repeating variable, as illustrated in Figure 10-4.

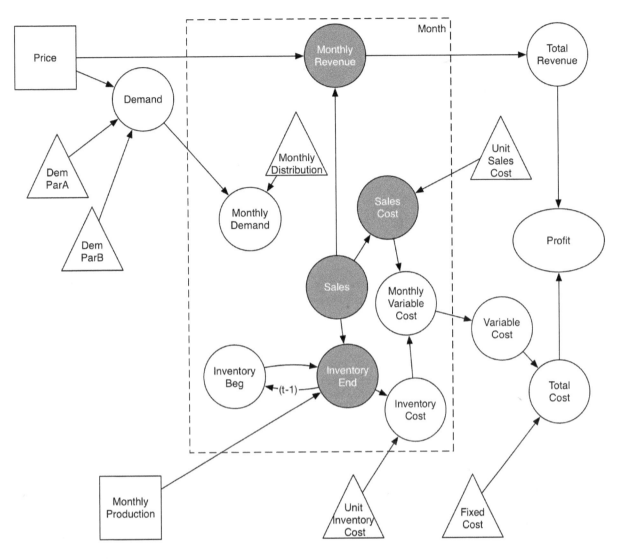

Figure 10-4 Calculating Monthly Revenue

As you can see, **Monthly Revenue** and **Total Revenue** are now calculated as shown below.

Variable	Type	Definition
Monthly Revenue	Calculated, Month	**Sales * Price**
Total Revenue	Calculated, Month	**SUM(Monthly Revenue)**

However, the diagram is not yet complete: **Sales** is not defined, and **Monthly Demand** influences no other variable. You have to find the relationship between these two variables. You know that **Sales** may, at times, equal **Monthly Demand**; but by definition it can't be higher than **Monthly Demand**.

When might it be lower? When Marco does not have enough products to sell. To address this situation, you can add the variable **Quantity Available** to our model, and define **Sales** as shown below.

Variable	Type	Definition
Sales	Calculated, Month	*MIN(Monthly Demand, Quantity Available)*

Figure 10-5 illustrates this formula.

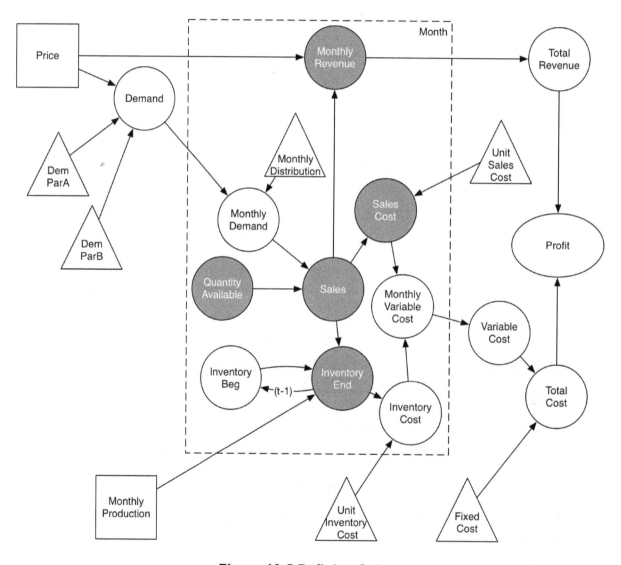

Figure 10-5 Defining Sales

At this point, how do you calculate *Quantity Available*? The number of widgets available for sale in any month is the number Marco has at the beginning of the month plus the number he produces in that month. So, you can calculate *Quantity Available* with the following formula.

Variable	Type	Definition
Quantity Available	Calculated, Month	*Inventory Beg + Monthly Production*

The final Formula Diagram is shown in Figure 10-6.

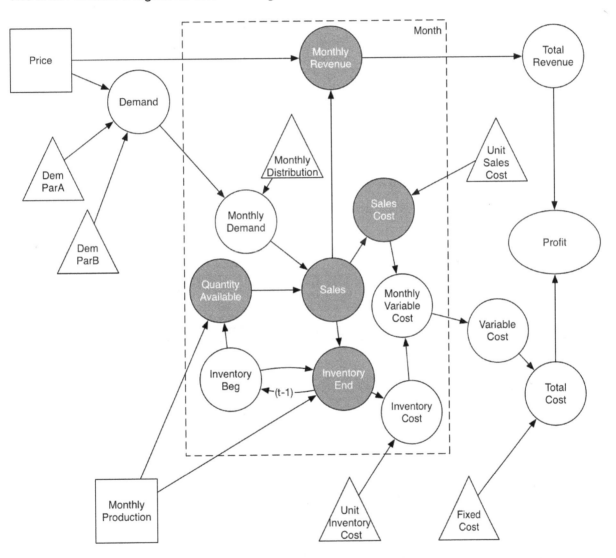

Figure 10-6 The Final Formula Diagram

Once more I'll update the Formula List, as shown in Table 10-1.

Table 10-1 Formula List, Revised Temporal Model

Variable	Type	Definition
Price	Input	**(To be set by user)**
Profit	Output	**Total Revenue – Total Cost**
DemParA	Data	**376,000**
DemParB	Data	**1.009**
Fixed Cost	Data	**$2,500,000**
Annual Demand	Calculated	**DemParA * DemParB^-Price**
Total Cost	Calculated	**Fixed Cost + Total Variable Cost**
Variable Cost	Calculated	**SUM(Monthly Variable Cost)**
Total Revenue	Calculated	**SUM(Monthly Revenue)**
Monthly Distribution	Data, Month	**Set of 12 values**
Monthly Production	Input	**(To be set by user)**
Unit Sales Cost	Data	**$150**
Unit Inventory Cost	Data	**$20**
Monthly Demand	Calculated, Month	**Annual Demand * Monthly Distribution**
Inventory End	Calculated, Month	**Inventory Beg + Monthly Production – Sales; Initial Inventory = 1,500**
Inventory Beg	Calculated, Month	**Inventory End(t−1)**
Inventory Cost	Calculated, Month	**Inventory End * Unit Inventory Cost**
Sales Cost	Calculated, Month	**Sales * Unit Sales Cost**
Monthly Variable Cost	Calculated, Month	**Inventory Cost + Sales Cost**
Monthly Revenue	Calculated, Month	**Sales * Price**
Sales	Calculated, Month	**MIN(Demand, Quantity Available)**
Quantity Available	Calculated, Month	**Inventory Beg + Monthly Production**

Modifying the Spreadsheet

Once you're satisfied with the modifications to the model, you can modify the spreadsheet as well to take those modifications into account, as well as the new formulas. Since you introduced three new variables (**Sales**, **Monthly Revenue** and **Quantity Available**), you now have three new definition blocks. You must also modify the formulas of the three variables affected by the changes: the variable **Sales** affects the **Sales Cost** definition block, and the **Inventory End** block; and **Monthly Revenue** affects the **Total Revenue** block.

You can add the variables in the order of their use. Since **Monthly Revenue** uses **Sales** and **Sales** uses **Quantity Available** but **Quantity Available** uses none of the added variables, you can start with that. (While definition blocks can be placed anywhere in the spreadsheet, it's best to locate them immediately after all the variables you need to reference.)

Let's start by inserting four rows after the definition block of **Inventory Beg**. Select *Rows 17 to 20* (as shown in Figure 10-7), and click the *Insert* icon of the *Home* tab.

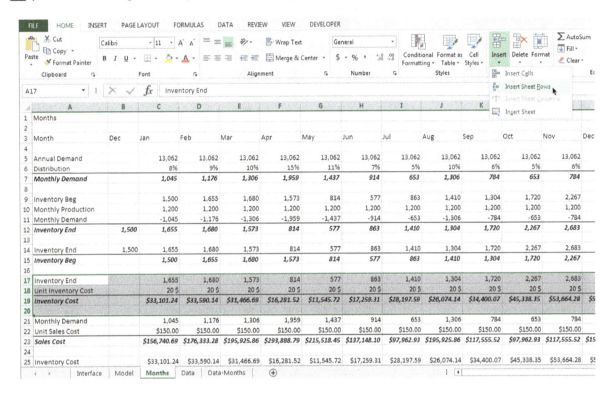

Figure 10-7 Inserting Rows for a New Block

You can then enter the definition block, naming the new variable and (as usual) drawing the separator line. This is shown in Figure 10-8.

C19			f_x	=SUM(C17:C18)			

	A	B	C	D	E	F	G
1	Months						
2							
3	Month	Dec	Jan	Feb	Mar	Apr	May
4							
5	Annual Demand		13,062	13,062	13,062	13,062	13,062
6	Distribution		8%	9%	10%	15%	11%
7	*Monthly Demand*		*1,045*	*1,176*	*1,306*	*1,959*	*1,437*
8							
9	Inventory Beg		1,500	1,655	1,680	1,573	814
10	Monthly Production		1,200	1,200	1,200	1,200	1,200
11	Monthly Demand		-1,045	-1,176	-1,306	-1,959	-1,437
12	*Inventory End*	*1,500*	*1,655*	*1,680*	*1,573*	*814*	*577*
13							
14	Inventory End	1,500	1,655	1,680	1,573	814	577
15	*Inventory Beg*		*1,500*	*1,655*	*1,680*	*1,573*	*814*
16							
17	Inventory Beg		1,500				
18	Monthly Production		1,200				
19	*Quantity Available*		*2,700*				
20							
21	Inventory End		1,655	1,680	1,573	814	577
22	Unit Inventory Cost		20 $	20 $	20 $	20 $	20 $
23	*Inventory Cost*		*$33,101.24*	*$33,590.14*	*$31,466.69*	*$16,281.52*	*$11,545.72*
24							
25	Monthly Demand		1,045	1,176	1,306	1,959	1,437
26	Unit Sales Cost		$150.00	$150.00	$150.00	$150.00	$150.00
27	*Sales Cost*		*$156,740.69*	*$176,333.28*	*$195,925.86*	*$293,888.79*	*$215,518.45*
28							

Interface | Model | **Months** | Data | Data-Months | ⊕

Figure 10-8 Definition Block for Quantity Available

Do the same for *Sales*: insert four lines and enter the definition block, as shown in Figure 10-9.

C23	▼	:	× ✓	f_x	=MIN(C21:C22)		

▲	A	B	C	D	E	F	G
1	Months						
2							
3	Month	Dec	Jan	Feb	Mar	Apr	May
4							
5	Annual Demand		13,062	13,062	13,062	13,062	13,062
6	Distribution		8%	9%	10%	15%	11%
7	*Monthly Demand*		*1,045*	*1,176*	*1,306*	*1,959*	*1,437*
8							
9	Inventory Beg		1,500	1,655	1,680	1,573	814
10	Monthly Production		1,200	1,200	1,200	1,200	1,200
11	Monthly Demand		-1,045	-1,176	-1,306	-1,959	-1,437
12	*Inventory End*	1,500	1,655	1,680	1,573	814	577
13							
14	Inventory End	1,500	1,655	1,680	1,573	814	577
15	*Inventory Beg*		1,500	1,655	1,680	1,573	814
16							
17	Inventory Beg		1,500				
18	Monthly Production		1,200				
19	*Quantity Available*		2,700				
20							
21	Monthly Demand		1,045				
22	Quantity Available		2,700				
23	*Sales*		*1,045*				
24							
25	Inventory End		1,655	1,680	1,573	814	577
26	Unit Inventory Cost		20 $	20 $	20 $	20 $	20 $
27	*Inventory Cost*		*$33,101.24*	*$33,590.14*	*$31,466.69*	*$16,281.52*	*$11,545.72*
28							

◄ ►	Interface	Model	**Months**	Data	Data-Months	⊕

Figure 10-9 Definition Block for Sales

Finally, create the definition block of *Monthly Revenue* in the last rows, as shown in Figure 10-10.

| | C39 | | ▾ | ⋮ | ✕ | ✓ | fx | =C37*C38 | |

▲	A	B	C	D	E	F	G
1	Months						
2							
3	Month	Dec	Jan	Feb	Mar	Apr	May
17	Inventory Beg		1,500				
18	Monthly Production		1,200				
19	*Quantity Available*		2,700				
20							
21	Monthly Demand		1,045				
22	Quantity Available		2,700				
23	*Sales*		1,045				
24							
25	Inventory End		1,655	1,680	1,573	814	577
26	Unit Inventory Cost		20 $	20 $	20 $	20 $	20 $
27	*Inventory Cost*		$33,101.24	$33,590.14	$31,466.69	$16,281.52	$11,545.72
28							
29	Monthly Demand		1,045	1,176	1,306	1,959	1,437
30	Unit Sales Cost		$150.00	$150.00	$150.00	$150.00	$150.00
31	*Sales Cost*		$156,740.69	$176,333.28	$195,925.86	$293,888.79	$215,518.45
32							
33	Inventory Cost		$33,101.24	$33,590.14	$31,466.69	$16,281.52	$11,545.72
34	Sales Cost		$156,740.69	$176,333.28	$195,925.86	$293,888.79	$215,518.45
35	*Monthly Variable Cost*		$189,841.93	$209,923.41	$227,392.55	$310,170.31	$227,064.17
36							
37	Sales		1,045				
38	Price		$375.00				
39	*Monthly Revenue*		$391,851.72				
40							
41							

| ◄ ► | Interface | Model | **Months** | Data | Data-Months | ⊕ |

Figure 10-10 Definition Block for Monthly Revenue

Having done all that, now you need to modify the definition blocks of *Inventory End* and *Sales Cost* so that they use the new variable *Sales* instead of *Monthly Demand*. You also need to change the label in <u>Column A</u> and the reference formula in <u>Column C</u>, but you do not have to change the definition formulas, because they correctly use the cells above them. This process is illustrated in Figure 10-11.

C29		▼	:	× ✓ *fx*	=Sales	

◢	A	B	C	D	E	F
1	Months					
2						
3	Month	Dec	Jan	Feb	Mar	Apr
4						
5	Annual Demand		13,062	13,062	13,062	13
6	Distribution		8%	9%	10%	
7	*Monthly Demand*		*1,045*	*1,176*	*1,306*	*1,*
8						
9	Inventory Beg		1,500	1,655	1,680	1
10	Monthly Production		1,200	1,200	1,200	1
11	Sales		-1,045	-1,176	-1,306	-1
12	*Inventory End*	*1,500*	*1,655*	*1,680*	*1,573*	
13						
14	Inventory End	1,500	1,655	1,680	1,573	
15	*Inventory Beg*		*1,500*	*1,655*	*1,680*	*1,*
16						
17	Inventory Beg		1,500			
18	Monthly Production		1,200			
19	*Quantity Available*		*2,700*			
20						
21	Monthly Demand		1,045			
22	Quantity Available		2,700			
23	*Sales*		*1,045*			
24						
25	Inventory End		1,655	1,680	1,573	
26	Unit Inventory Cost		20 $	20 $	20 $	
27	*Inventory Cost*		*$33,101.24*	*$33,590.14*	*$31,466.69*	*$16,28:*
28						
29	Sales		1,045	1,176	1,306	1
30	Unit Sales Cost		$150.00	$150.00	$150.00	$15
31	*Sales Cost*		*$156,740.69*	*$176,333.28*	*$195,925.86*	*$293,88:*
32						
33	Inventory Cost		$33,101.24	$33,590.14	$31,466.69	$16,28
34	Sales Cost		$156,740.69	$176,333.28	$195,925.86	$293,88
35	*Monthly Variable Cost*		*$189,841.93*	*$209,923.41*	*$227,392.55*	*$310,17(*
36						
37	Sales		1,045			
38	Price		$375.00			
39	*Monthly Revenue*		*$391,851.72*			

◄ ► | Interface | Model | **Months** | Data | Data-Months | ⊕

Figure 10-11 Modifying Definition Blocks, Inventory End and Sales Cost

Figure 10-12 shows the formula view of the modified model.

Figure 10-12 Formula View of the Modified Model

You finish modifying the **Months** sheet by copying the whole modified model in *Column C* into the other 11 months—as shown in Figure 10-13.

	A	B	C	D	E	F	G	H	I	J	K	L	M	N
1	Months													
2														
3	Month	Dec	Jan	Feb	Mar	Apr	May	Jun	Jul	Aug	Sep	Oct	Nov	Dec
4														
5	Annual Demand		13,062	13,062	13,062	13,062	13,062	13,062	13,062	13,062	13,062	13,062	13,062	13,062
6	Distribution		8%	9%	10%	15%	11%	7%	5%	10%	6%	5%	6%	8%
7	*Monthly Demand*		*1,045*	*1,176*	*1,306*	*1,959*	*1,437*	*914*	*653*	*1,306*	*784*	*653*	*784*	*1,045*
8														
9	Inventory Beg		1,500	1,655	1,680	1,573	814	577	863	1,410	1,304	1,720	2,267	2,683
10	Monthly Production		1,200	1,200	1,200	1,200	1,200	1,200	1,200	1,200	1,200	1,200	1,200	1,200
11	Sales		-1,045	-1,176	-1,306	-1,959	-1,437	-914	-653	-1,306	-784	-653	-784	-1,045
12	*Inventory End*	1,500	*1,655*	*1,680*	*1,573*	*814*	*577*	*863*	*1,410*	*1,304*	*1,720*	*2,267*	*2,683*	*2,838*
13														
14	Inventory End	1,500	1,655	1,680	1,573	814	577	863	1,410	1,304	1,720	2,267	2,683	2,838
15	*Inventory Beg*		*1,500*	*1,655*	*1,680*	*1,573*	*814*	*577*	*863*	*1,410*	*1,304*	*1,720*	*2,267*	*2,683*
16														
17	Inventory Beg		1,500	1,655	1,680	1,573	814	577	863	1,410	1,304	1,720	2,267	2,683
18	Monthly Production		1,200	1,200	1,200	1,200	1,200	1,200	1,200	1,200	1,200	1,200	1,200	1,200
19	*Quantity Available*		*2,700*	*2,855*	*2,880*	*2,773*	*2,014*	*1,777*	*2,063*	*2,610*	*2,504*	*2,920*	*3,467*	*3,883*
20														
21	Monthly Demand		1,045	1,176	1,306	1,959	1,437	914	653	1,306	784	653	784	1,045
22	Quantity Available		2,700	2,855	2,880	2,773	2,014	1,777	2,063	2,610	2,504	2,920	3,467	3,883
23	*Sales*		*1,045*	*1,176*	*1,306*	*1,959*	*1,437*	*914*	*653*	*1,306*	*784*	*653*	*784*	*1,045*
24														
25	Inventory End		1,655	1,680	1,573	814	577	863	1,410	1,304	1,720	2,267	2,683	2,838
26	Unit Inventory Cost		20 $	20 $	20 $	20 $	20 $	20 $	20 $	20 $	20 $	20 $	20 $	20 $
27	*Inventory Cost*		*$33,101.24*	*$33,590.14*	*$31,466.69*	*$16,281.52*	*$11,545.72*	*$17,259.31*	*$28,197.59*	*$26,074.14*	*$34,400.07*	*$45,338.35*	*$53,664.28*	*$56,765.52*
28														
29	Sales		1,045	1,176	1,306	1,959	1,437	914	653	1,306	784	653	784	1,045
30	Unit Sales Cost		$150.00	$150.00	$150.00	$150.00	$150.00	$150.00	$150.00	$150.00	$150.00	$150.00	$150.00	$150.00
31	*Sales Cost*		*$156,740.69*	*$176,333.28*	*$195,925.86*	*$293,888.79*	*$215,518.45*	*$137,148.10*	*$97,962.93*	*$195,925.86*	*$117,555.52*	*$97,962.93*	*$117,555.52*	*$156,740.69*
32														
33	Inventory Cost		$33,101.24	$33,590.14	$31,466.69	$16,281.52	$11,545.72	$17,259.31	$28,197.59	$26,074.14	$34,400.07	$45,338.35	$53,664.28	$56,765.52
34	Sales Cost		$156,740.69	$176,333.28	$195,925.86	$293,888.79	$215,518.45	$137,148.10	$97,962.93	$195,925.86	$117,555.52	$97,962.93	$117,555.52	$156,740.69
35	*Monthly Variable Cost*		*$189,841.93*	*$209,923.41*	*$227,392.55*	*$310,170.31*	*$227,064.17*	*$154,407.41*	*$126,160.52*	*$222,000.00*	*$151,955.59*	*$143,301.28*	*$171,219.79*	*$213,506.21*
36														
37	Sales		1,045	1,176	1,306	1,959	1,437	914	653	1,306	784	653	784	1,045
38	Price		$375.00	$375.00	$375.00	$375.00	$375.00	$375.00	$375.00	$375.00	$375.00	$375.00	$375.00	$375.00
39	*Monthly Revenue*		*$391,851.72*	*$440,833.19*	*$489,814.65*	*$734,721.98*	*$538,796.12*	*$342,870.26*	*$244,907.33*	*$489,814.65*	*$293,888.79*	*$244,907.33*	*$293,888.79*	*$391,851.72*

Interface | Model | **Months** | Data | Data-Months

Figure 10-13 Copying the Modified Month in All Time Periods

To finish, you modify the definition of *Total Revenue* in the **Model** sheet. Since the new definition of *Total Revenue* now involves a repeating variable, you'll want to insert its definition block just after the reference to the repeating entity *Month*. Your first step is to delete the 4 rows of the old definition block, including the blank separating row, as shown in Figure 10-14. (Note that after you do this, the variable *Total Revenue* becomes undefined, and this shows as a *#REF!* error in the definition block of *Profit*. This error will disappear automatically when you re-create the name of *Total Revenue*.)

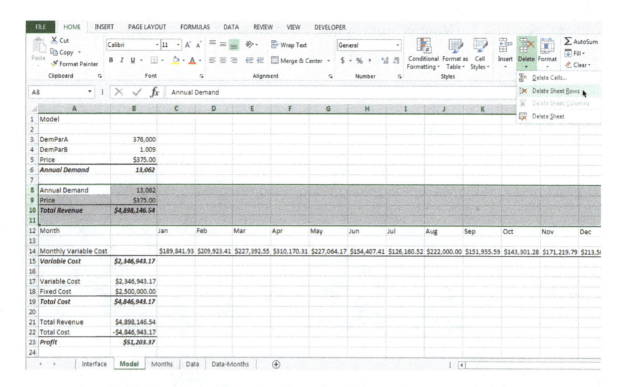

Figure 10-14 Deleting the Old Total Revenue Definition Block

You now insert three rows for the new *Total Revenue* definition block, as shown in Figure 10-15.

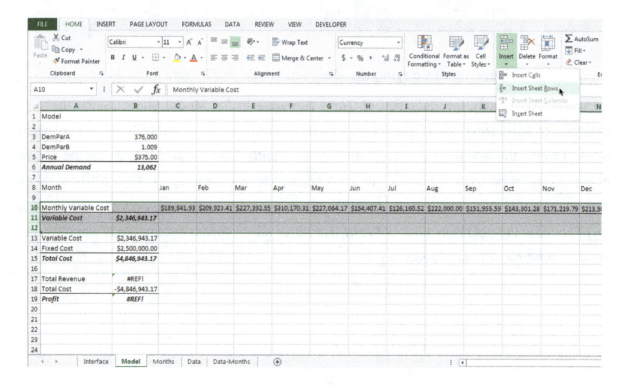

Figure 10-15 Inserting a New Total Revenue Definition Block

Now enter the definition block of *Total Revenue* as you did for *Monthly Variable Cost*. When you name the variable, the #REF! error that appeared in the *Profit* block will go away—as shown in Figure 10-16. If it doesn't go away, it may be due to a slight difference in the name of the new variable: make sure you wrote it exactly as it was before.

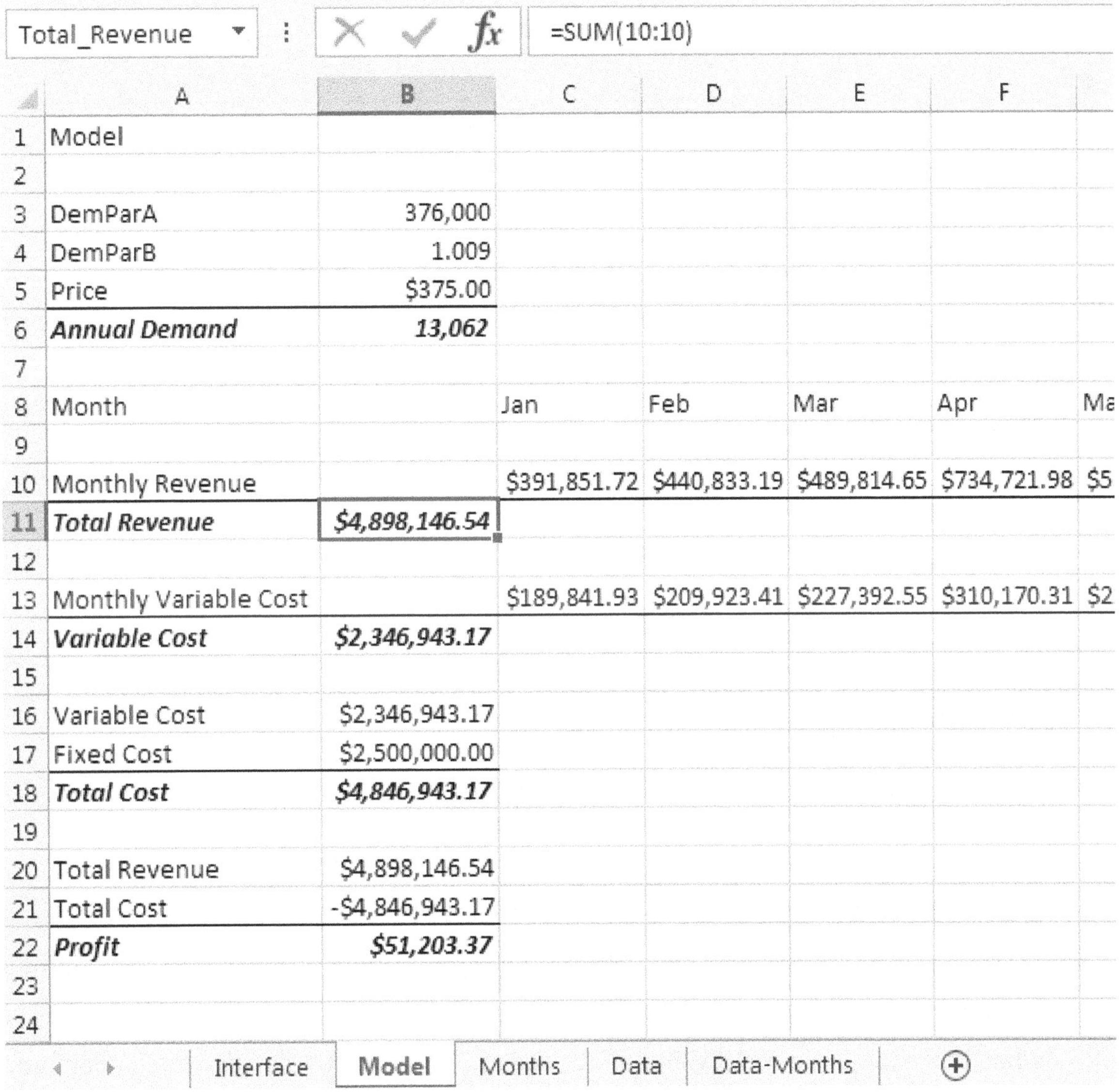

	A	B	C	D	E	F
	Total_Revenue ▾ : ✕ ✓ *fx* =SUM(10:10)					
1	Model					
2						
3	DemParA	376,000				
4	DemParB	1.009				
5	Price	$375.00				
6	*Annual Demand*	13,062				
7						
8	Month		Jan	Feb	Mar	Apr	Ma
9						
10	Monthly Revenue		$391,851.72	$440,833.19	$489,814.65	$734,721.98	$5
11	*Total Revenue*	$4,898,146.54				
12						
13	Monthly Variable Cost		$189,841.93	$209,923.41	$227,392.55	$310,170.31	$2
14	*Variable Cost*	$2,346,943.17				
15						
16	Variable Cost	$2,346,943.17				
17	Fixed Cost	$2,500,000.00				
18	*Total Cost*	$4,846,943.17				
19						
20	Total Revenue	$4,898,146.54				
21	Total Cost	-$4,846,943.17				
22	*Profit*	$51,203.37				
23						
24						

Interface | **Model** | Months | Data | Data-Months | ⊕

Figure 10-16 The New Total Revenue Definition Block

How can you test your modifications? If you look back at *Row 23* of Figure 10-13, you can see that *Sales* is always equal to *Monthly Demand*—so the effect of your actions can't be seen. But if you change the value of *Monthly Production*, you can see some months where the demand is not wholly satisfied.

By changing the value from *1,200* to *800* in the **Interface** sheet, as shown in Figure 10-17, you can see that in a few months (April, May, June, September and December), *Sales* is equal to *Quantity Available* instead of *Monthly Demand*. This confirms that the model is behaving correctly.

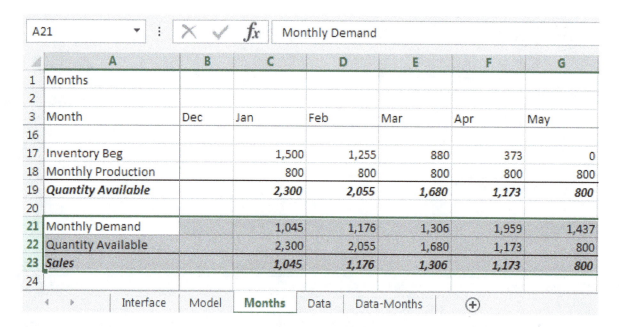

Figure 10-17 Testing the Modified Model

Chapter 10 Overview

Here are the main points for you to remember from Chapter 10.

- You must ensure that any modifications are made to all three elements: the Formula List, the Formula Diagram and the spreadsheet itself.

- If you need to change the logic behind an integral part of the model, the Formula Diagram helps you to easily conceptualize the change—and lets you see what is (or what could be) affected by the modification. This makes its implementation quite straightforward.

- Generally, all spreadsheet modifications are made in a single column—the first column of the repeating model. Then the entire column is copied over across the number of instances. (This makes it hard to forget to copy a modified formula, since you do this operation just once, at the end of the process.)

In Chapter 11, you'll learn about modelling techniques, including modelling special cases.

Chapter 11   Using Advanced Modelling Techniques

How to use this chapter

This chapter is a leisurely read. But it's not light reading: it shows how to use special purpose variables to model special cases. Allow about 30 minutes for the first time you read it, and come back to it when you need to use one the techniques for the first time.

The key to developing a good repeating sub-model is building a model that's valid for all instances of a repeating entity. It's important that you not program exceptions into the model to influence its behaviour. Rather, you should transform any exceptions into a regular situation by carefully choosing values for repeating data variables.

Modelling Special Cases

In some irregular cases, one or more instances of a repeating entity does not follow the same rules as the others. In the case of Marco's Widgets model with regions from Chapter 5, for example, there might be a special tax levied only in the East region. To model this fact, you might think of using an IF function, as defined in this formula:

Tax = IF(Region= "East," Special Tax, 0).

The problem with this approach is that the formula contains the constant ***East***—and constants in formulas complicate future maintenance. There may still be problems even if you create a new data variable, ***Special Tax Region***, and change the formula to:

Tax = IF(Region=Special Tax Region, Special Tax, 0)

In this case, you assign the value ***East*** to the new data variable. But what would happen if another region also imposed a special tax? What would happen if the tax rate in the other regions was different? Obviously, these would require complex IF functions.

Similarly, looking at Marco's temporal model from Chapter 8, if you want to model an increase in inventory cost starting in October, you might use the formula:

Monthly Unit Inventory Cost =
IF(Month>=10, Unit Inventory Cost, Unit Inventory Cost + Cost Increase).

However, this is also problematic, for two reasons. First, the formula mixes an operator and a function, which goes against the Simplicity Rule. Second, it's not flexible. What would happen if the increase in monthly inventory cost changed, or if the increase was spread gradually over a few months?

Luckily, there is a simple solution to these problems. You just approach all irregular cases as if they were regular, and as if they existed for all instances of a repeating entity. But if you create a variable to handle such a case, it's important that you apply it to all instances of the repeating entity.

You must choose which approach you prefer: either a single value used consistently in all instances, or a set of values with one value for each and every instance.

This rule lets you avoid the use of an *IF* function to treat irregular cases. In our first example of Marco's regional model from Chapter 5, to model the special tax, you start with the original model, re-illustrated in Figure 11-1.

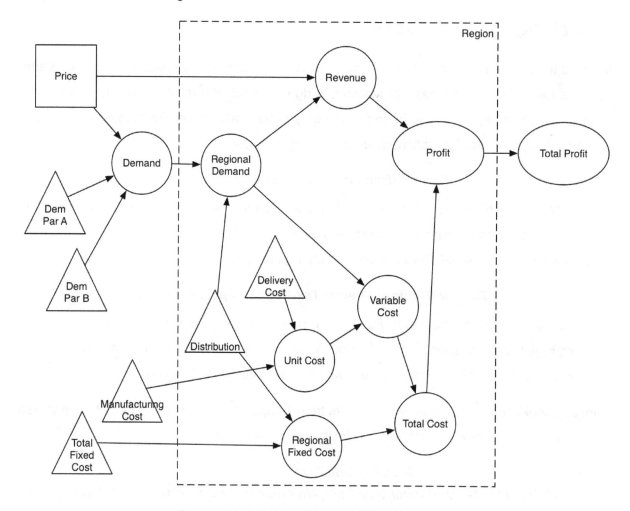

Figure 11-1 Original Model With Regions

Then you introduce a multi-value data variable, **Special Tax** (with values of 0%, 5% and 0%). This data variable, used with **Regional Demand**, calculates the **Tax** variable with the following formula:

Tax = Regional Demand * Special Tax.

You can see the new variable in Figure 11-2.

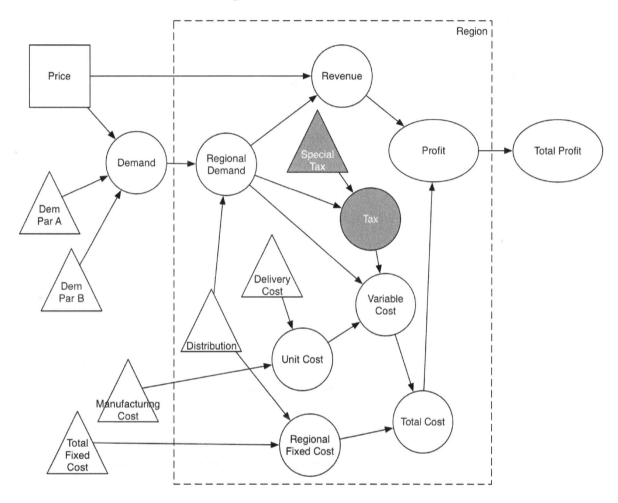

Figure 11-2 Modified Model, Special Tax

Where in the diagram do you specify that the special tax is only for the East region? The answer is *Nowhere*. The model describes the calculations that need to be made in each region, and you do not model exceptions. In the **Data** sheet, you specify that the **Special Tax** is only for the **East** region. In fact, this approach also allows you to specify different tax rates for different regions, making it more flexible. You do not need to change the formulas if the situation changes.

There are three different ways of modelling special cases. These are often interchangeable, and you can select the one that best suits the way the data is presented. These three approaches involve different types of data variable:

- an **indicator** data variable,
- a **distribution** data variable,
- an **allocation** data variable.

To illustrate these approaches, let's consider a new case: Josie is a student and she wants to model her budget for the next school year. Among the activities the model has to track are her incomes and expenses:

- $2,250 in tuition fees, spread over three payments ($950 each in September and January, and the remaining $350 in June);
- a student loan of $2,915 she will receive in October;
- a $2,085 scholarship she will receive (in three equal parts in November, January and March).

Using an Indicator Data Variable

This is a repeating data variable to which you assign the value 1 when the modelled event does occur, and the value 0 when it doesn't occur. The multi-value indicator data variable is usually accompanied by a single-value data variable to calculate the repeating calculated variable to be used for each instance. To calculate this, you simply multiply the indicator data variable and the single-value data variable. Since the indicator is always either 0 or 1, the repeating calculated variable takes the value of the single-value data variable when the indicator is 1, and the value 0 otherwise.

In Josie's budget, you use *Loan Indicator* as the indicator data variable, *Loan Amount* as the value to be used, and *Loan* as the amount she'll receive every month. Figure 11-3 illustrates the model portion.

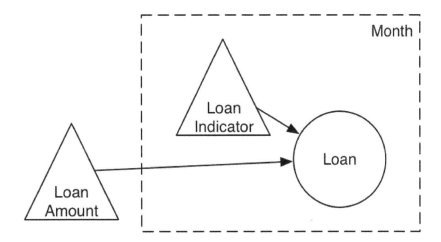

Figure 11-3 Modelling With an Indicator Data Variable

Figure 11-4 shows how *Loan Amount* is defined in the **Data** sheet and Figure 11-5 shows how *Loan Indicator* is defined in the **Data-Months** sheet.

A9	▼	:	✕	✓	*fx*	Loan Amount

⊿	A	B	C	D	E
1	Data				
2					
3	*Rent*	300 $			
4	*Telephone*	40 $			
5	*Transport*	50 $			
6	*Weekly Groceries*	42 $			
7	*Minimum Balance*	300 $			
8	*Initial Balance*	250 $			
9	*Loan Amount*	2,915 $			
10	*Scholarship Amount*	2,085 $			
11	*Electricity Amount*	250 $			
12	*Book Amount*	300 $			
13	*Weekly Full Time Pay*	300 $			
14	*Weekly Part Time Pay*	85 $			

◄	►	...	Interface	Model	Months	**Data**	Data-Months

Figure 11-4 The Loan Amount Data Variable Definition

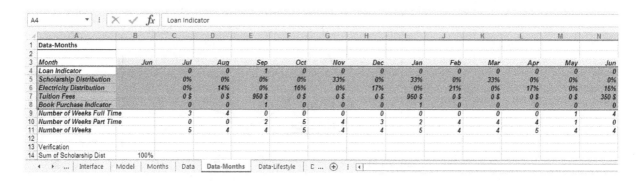

Figure 11-5 The Loan Indicator Data Variable Definition

Finally, Figure 11-6 shows how **Loan** is calculated in the **Months** sheet.

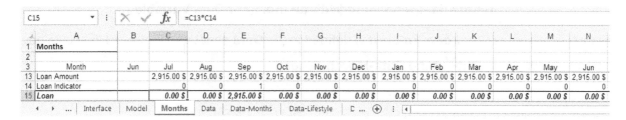

Figure 11-6 The Loan Calculated Variable Definition

Using a Distribution Data Variable

The second way of modelling irregular cases is to define a distribution data variable that indicates the proportion of a single-value amount data variable associated with each instance of the repeating entity. The distribution data variable must add up to 100%. As with the indicator data variable, you create a repeating calculated variable to find the value associated with each instance. The formula is the product of the multi-value distribution data variable and the single-value amount data variable.

In Josie's case, you're told that the scholarship will be paid in three equal instalments: in November, January and March. As shown in Figure 11-7, you model this with a multi-value data variable, **Scholarship Distribution**, a single-value data variable, **Scholarship Amount**; and a repeating calculated variable, **Scholarship**.

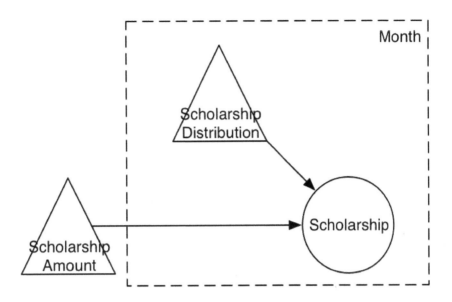

Figure 11-7 Distribution Data Variable

To implement this, you create a repeating data variable, **Scholarship Distribution**. It has the value of one-third of the total scholarship amount in the specified three months, and 0 in all the others. You also create a single-value data variable for the **Scholarship Amount** ($2,085). The two data variables are illustrated in *Row 10* of Figure 11-4 and *Row 5* of Figure 11-5.

The calculation of **Scholarship** is shown in row 11 of Figure 11-8.

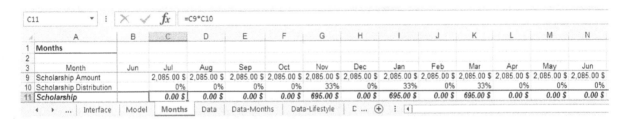

	A	B	C	D	E	F	G	H	I	J	K	L	M	N
1	Months													
2														
3	Month	Jun	Jul	Aug	Sep	Oct	Nov	Dec	Jan	Feb	Mar	Apr	May	Jun
9	Scholarship Amount		2,085.00 $	2,085.00 $	2,085.00 $	2,085.00 $	2,085.00 $	2,085.00 $	2,085.00 $	2,085.00 $	2,085.00 $	2,085.00 $	2,085.00 $	2,085.00 $
10	Scholarship Distribution		0%	0%	0%	0%	33%	0%	33%	0%	33%	0%	0%	0%
11	Scholarship		0.00 $	0.00 $	0.00 $	0.00 $	695.00 $	0.00 $	695.00 $	0.00 $	695.00 $	0.00 $	0.00 $	0.00 $

C11 — =C9*C10

Interface | Model | Months | Data | Data-Months | Data-Lifestyle | D ...

Figure 11-8 Scholarship Calculation

Using an Allocation Data Variable

The third way of modelling an irregular case is to simply create a repeating data variable, entering the appropriate values in each instance. There is no need to create additional variables. In Josie's case, you model **Tuition Fees** this way, as illustrated in Figure 11-9.

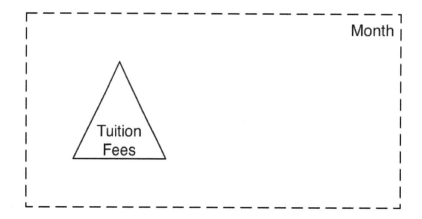

Figure 11-9 Modelling an Allocation Data Variable

Its implementation is illustrated in Row 7 of Figure 11-5.

Finally, Figure 11-10 illustrates how to use the three irregular case variables in the temporal model. You can see **Scholarship** and **Loan** in *Rows 30 and 31*, and **Tuition Fees** in *Row 43*. You can also see other irregular case variables like **Books**, defined in *Row 36* and used in *Row 42*, and **Electricity**, defined in *Row 40* and used in *Row 44*.

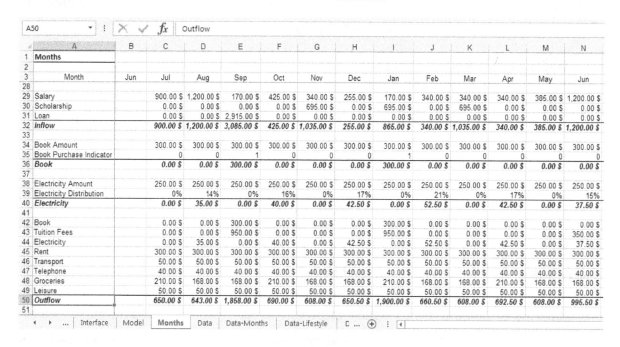

A50		fx	Outflow											
	A	B	C	D	E	F	G	H	I	J	K	L	M	N
1	**Months**													
2														
3	Month	Jun	Jul	Aug	Sep	Oct	Nov	Dec	Jan	Feb	Mar	Apr	May	Jun
28														
29	Salary		900.00 $	1,200.00 $	170.00 $	425.00 $	340.00 $	255.00 $	170.00 $	340.00 $	340.00 $	340.00 $	385.00 $	1,200.00 $
30	Scholarship		0.00 $	0.00 $	0.00 $	0.00 $	695.00 $	0.00 $	695.00 $	0.00 $	695.00 $	0.00 $	0.00 $	0.00 $
31	Loan		0.00 $	0.00 $	2,915.00 $	0.00 $	0.00 $	0.00 $	0.00 $	0.00 $	0.00 $	0.00 $	0.00 $	0.00 $
32	*Inflow*		*900.00 $*	*1,200.00 $*	*3,085.00 $*	*425.00 $*	*1,035.00 $*	*255.00 $*	*865.00 $*	*340.00 $*	*1,035.00 $*	*340.00 $*	*385.00 $*	*1,200.00 $*
33														
34	Book Amount		300.00 $	300.00 $	300.00 $	300.00 $	300.00 $	300.00 $	300.00 $	300.00 $	300.00 $	300.00 $	300.00 $	300.00 $
35	Book Purchase Indicator		0	0	1	0	0	0	0	1	0	0	0	0
36	*Book*		*0.00 $*	*0.00 $*	*300.00 $*	*0.00 $*	*0.00 $*	*0.00 $*	*300.00 $*	*0.00 $*	*0.00 $*	*0.00 $*	*0.00 $*	*0.00 $*
37														
38	Electricity Amount		250.00 $	250.00 $	250.00 $	250.00 $	250.00 $	250.00 $	250.00 $	250.00 $	250.00 $	250.00 $	250.00 $	250.00 $
39	Electricity Distribution		0%	14%	0%	16%	0%	17%	0%	21%	0%	17%	0%	15%
40	*Electricity*		*0.00 $*	*35.00 $*	*0.00 $*	*40.00 $*	*0.00 $*	*42.50 $*	*0.00 $*	*52.50 $*	*0.00 $*	*42.50 $*	*0.00 $*	*37.50 $*
41														
42	Book		0.00 $	0.00 $	300.00 $	0.00 $	0.00 $	0.00 $	300.00 $	0.00 $	0.00 $	0.00 $	0.00 $	0.00 $
43	Tuition Fees		0.00 $	0.00 $	950.00 $	0.00 $	0.00 $	0.00 $	950.00 $	0.00 $	0.00 $	0.00 $	0.00 $	350.00 $
44	Electricity		0.00 $	35.00 $	0.00 $	40.00 $	0.00 $	42.50 $	0.00 $	52.50 $	0.00 $	42.50 $	0.00 $	37.50 $
45	Rent		300.00 $	300.00 $	300.00 $	300.00 $	300.00 $	300.00 $	300.00 $	300.00 $	300.00 $	300.00 $	300.00 $	300.00 $
46	Transport		50.00 $	50.00 $	50.00 $	50.00 $	50.00 $	50.00 $	50.00 $	50.00 $	50.00 $	50.00 $	50.00 $	50.00 $
47	Telephone		40.00 $	40.00 $	40.00 $	40.00 $	40.00 $	40.00 $	40.00 $	40.00 $	40.00 $	40.00 $	40.00 $	40.00 $
48	Groceries		210.00 $	168.00 $	168.00 $	210.00 $	168.00 $	168.00 $	210.00 $	168.00 $	168.00 $	210.00 $	168.00 $	168.00 $
49	Leisure		50.00 $	50.00 $	50.00 $	50.00 $	50.00 $	50.00 $	50.00 $	50.00 $	50.00 $	50.00 $	50.00 $	50.00 $
50	*Outflow*		*650.00 $*	*643.00 $*	*1,858.00 $*	*690.00 $*	*608.00 $*	*650.50 $*	*1,900.00 $*	*660.50 $*	*608.00 $*	*692.50 $*	*608.00 $*	*995.50 $*
51														

Interface | Model | Months | Data | Data-Months | Data-Lifestyle | D ...

Figure 11-10 Irregular Case Variables

Using a Calculated Indicator Variable

When you first develop a model, you may not know for sure when certain future events will happen. In an inventory model, for example, you don't yet know when it will be time to order more stock from the supplier. You model such situations very like the repeating indicator data variables, with this difference: the 0 or 1 value is not an input, but a repeating calculated variable—determined by a certain condition. To do this, you use a simple *IF* function:

IF(condition, 1, 0).

For example, in inventory management you use a **reorder point**. If the quantity you have in inventory falls below that point, it's time to reorder the product. The condition to set the reorder indicator to 1 is then:

Inventory End <= Reorder Point.

Otherwise, the indicator is set to 0. Figure 11-11 illustrates how you model this situation.

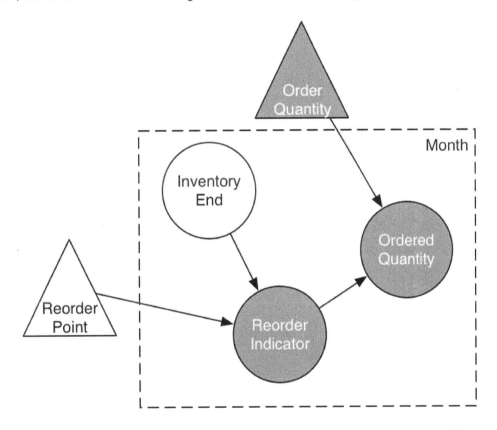

Figure 11-11 Modelling a Repeating Calculated Indicator Variable

The formulas associated with this portion of the model are:

Reorder Indicator = IF(Inventory End <= Reorder Point, 1, 0)

*Ordered Quantity = Order Quantity * Reorder Indicator*

A calculated indicator variable has another useful quality. Since its value is 1 only whenever the event occurs, and is otherwise 0, its sum tells you the number of times the event has occurred in the model. From this, you can create a single-value variable that calculates the number of times you'll have to re-order. The formula is:

Number of Orders = Sum(Reorder Indicator)

This new variable, in turn, could be used to calculate total order costs.

The advantage of using the special-case techniques described here is that your model is flexible and easy to maintain. You develop it as if there were no irregular events, and let the user enter the proper data variable values to specify when those events do occur.

Using a State Indicator Variable

The difference between an event indicator variable and a state indicator variable is that an event occurs in only one period, whereas a state may last for many periods. For example, "Vacation Starts" is an event; "On Vacation" is a state. Another difference is that a state is a binary concept: you're either in the condition, or out of it. When you're in a state, your model should behave differently than when you're out of it. Here are a few examples of states.

- If a machine is under repair for some period, during this time production capacity is reduced.
- If an employee is away, some activities take longer to perform.
- If a price reduction is offered for a certain period, price goes down and demand goes up.

Using State Variables

You can model a state with four or five indicator variables, and at least two formulas. First, you need two event indicator variables to indicate the start of state event and the end of state event. Like all indicator variables, these have a value of either 0 or 1. They can either be data variables entered by the user, or calculated variables. For these, you must create formulas to determine their values.

To model a state with a formula similar to the inventory formula, you need to track two things: the state at the beginning of each period, and at the end of it. Using two indicator variables, ***State Beg*** and ***State End***, you calculate the two state-indicator variables using these formulas:

State End = State Beg + Start of State – End of State

$$State\ Beg = State\ End(t–1).$$

When you develop a model, you must always be careful to assign the value 1 to **Start of State** and **End of State** in an alternating sequence. You can't have the **Start of State** of two periods taking the value 1, without **End of State** taking the value 1 between them (since this would produce a value greater than 1 for **State End**).

Similarly, you can't have the **End of State** of two periods taking the value 1 without **Start of State** taking the value 1 between them, as this would produce a negative value for **State End**.

One way of making sure that you can't start a state while it's currently in use is to create another variable, named **Start of State Needed**, to determine whether a start is actually needed. This allows you to set **Start of State** to *1*, if it's needed, and if the state is not currently "on." For this, you need these two formulas:

Start of State Needed = IF(whatever condition needs to be checked, 1, 0)

Start of State = IF(Start of State Needed =1 AND State Beg =0, 1, 0)

The second formula ensures that **Start of State** and **State Beg** are never equal to 1 in the same period—meaning that **State End** will never be bigger than 1.

Example: Using State Indicator Variables

To illustrate the use of state indicator variables, let's look at a company that sells construction equipment online. It offers a delivery service for its clients, and needs to keep track of the costs of this—specifically, the cost of regular maintenance of its delivery truck.

Maintenance is performed several times a year, whenever the trip odometer reaches 15,000 km, and the truck is in the garage for two weeks (the trip odometer is then reset to 0). During this two-week period, the company must rent a vehicle for its deliveries, which is more costly.

The company knows the frequency of maintenance, and the normal weekly distance driven by its truck. These data variables make it possible to calculate variables such as **Distance Driven** and **Maintenance Needed**. The partial Formula Diagram is illustrated in Figure 11-12.

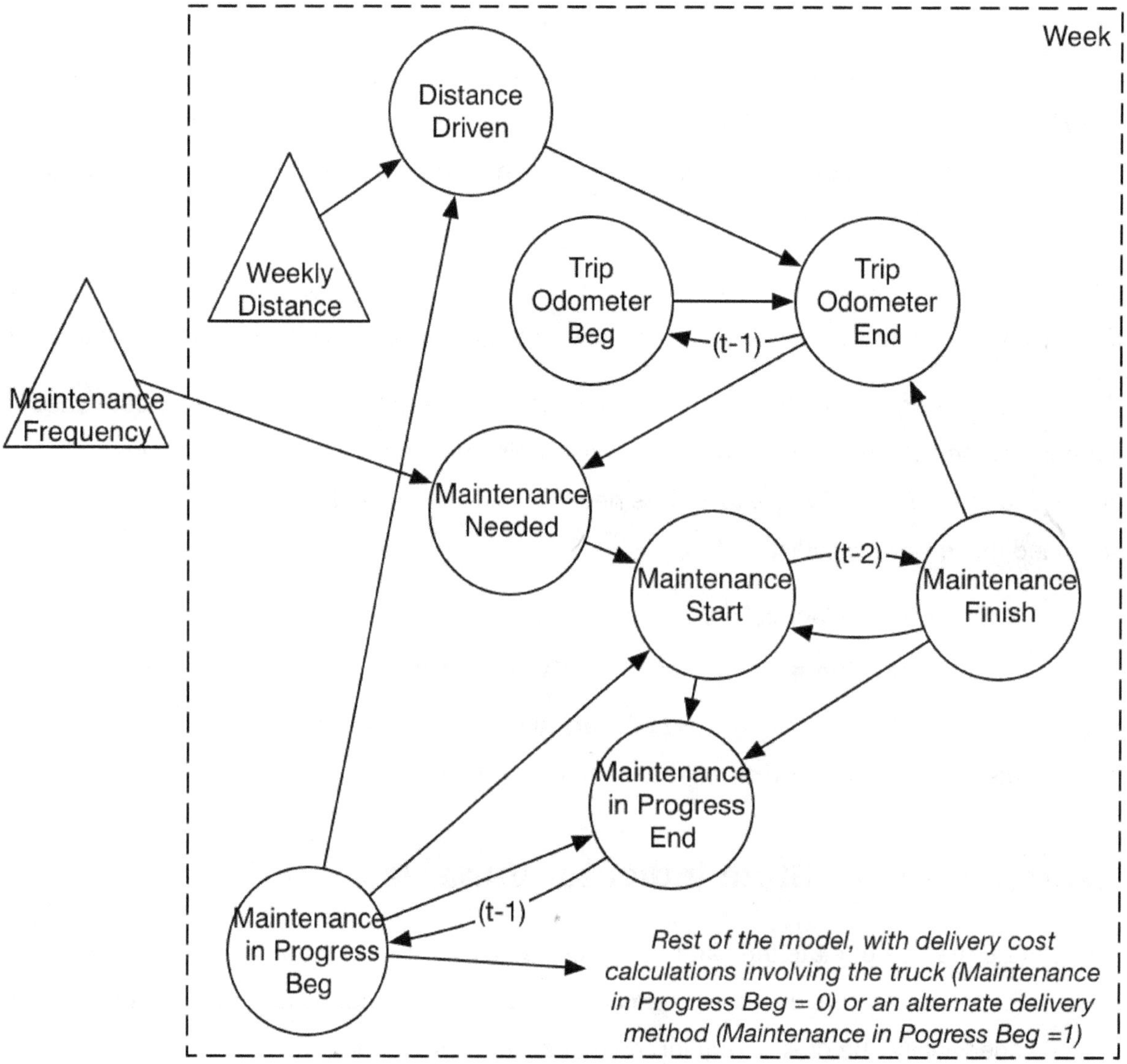
Week
Distance Driven
Weekly Distance
Maintenance Frequency
Trip Odometer Beg
Trip Odometer End
(t-1)
Maintenance Needed
Maintenance Start
(t-2)
Maintenance Finish
Maintenance in Progress End
(t-1)
Maintenance in Progress Beg
Rest of the model, with delivery cost calculations involving the truck (Maintenance in Progress Beg = 0) or an alternate delivery method (Maintenance in Pogress Beg =1)

Figure 11-12 Example of State Indicator Variables

The Formula List is shown in Table 11-1.

Table 11-1 State Indicator Variables

Variable	Type	Formula
Weekly Distance	Data, Week	***(To be set by user)***
Maintenance Frequency	Data	***(To be set by user)***
Distance Driven	Calculated, Week	***IF(Maintenance Indicator Beg = 1, 0, Weekly Distance)***
Trip Odometer End	Calculated, Week	***IF(Maintenance Finished =1, 0,Trip Odometer Beg + Distance Driven)***

Variable	Type	Formula
Trip Odometer Beg	Calculated, Week	*Trip Odometer End(t–1)*
Maintenance Needed	Calculated, Week	*IF(Trip Odometer End >= Maintenance Frequency, 1, 0)*
Maintenance Start	Calculated, Week	*IF(Maintenance Needed = 1 AND Maintenance in Progress Beg = 0, 1, 0)*
Maintenance Finish	Calculated, Week	*Maintenance Start(t–2)*
Maintenance in Progress End	Calculated, Week	*Maintenance in Progress Beg + Maintenance Start – Maintenance Finish*
Maintenance in Progress Beg	Calculated, Week	*Maintenance in Progress End(t–1)*

Since you have a *(t–2)* reference here, the temporal model will have two initialization periods, *Weeks* numbered *-1* and *0*. The user needs to supply an initial value for *Trip Odometer End* for *Week 0*, and two initial values for *Maintenance Start* for *Weeks -1* and *0*. As the developer, you must also initialize the variable *Maintenance in Progress End* in *Week 0*. For this, you have two choices:

- you supply an initial value—in which case you run the risk of having an inconsistent initial situation (such as *Maintenance Start* of *Week 0* set to *1*, and *Maintenance in Progress End* of *Week 0* set to *0*);
- you define formulas in the initialization columns to ensure that the value of *Maintenance Indicator End* is always correct.

Obviously, the latter option is preferable.

Looking Forward in Time

Sometimes your actions today are based on a result you expect in the next period. This can be modelled with a *(t+1)* reference, requiring you to supply a finalization value for the variables involved.

A common concept in inventory management is "safety stock"—a way of ensuring that a company has enough product in stock, at the end of the current period, for at least the early sales of the next period. The company may decide to end each month with a safety stock equivalent to 25% of the next month's expected demand. So if it expects to sell 200 items next month, it will want 50 items in stock at the end of this month. This leads to the two following formulas:

Inventory End = Demand Next Month * Target Stock Percentage

Demand Next Month = Demand(t+1)

What does this do to your usual inventory formula? Well, it can be used to calculate another variable. If you start with:

Inventory End = Inventory Beg + Production – Sales,

you can determine Production with the formula:

Production = Inventory End + Sales – Inventory Beg

This sets the value of this month's Production to a value that ensures that the company ends the month with the required quantity.

Chapter 11 Overview

Here are the main points for you to remember from Chapter 11.

- Don't use exceptions for special cases; just treat them as though they can occur for all instances. Manage the exceptions with the values of your data variables.
- Recognize when to use indicator variables and apply them correctly.
- You may need to refer to several periods in the past, or periods in the future.

Chapter 12 introduces you to some strategies for spreadsheet management.

Chapter 12   Managing Spreadsheets

How to use this chapter

This chapter is a leisurely read. It discusses various issues regarding the management of your spreadsheets. Allow 15 minutes.

This chapter addresses basic approaches to the management and maintenance of spreadsheets, focusing on verification—in the hope that you'll be able to avoid that 90% error rate. This body of knowledge isn't one you can pick up quickly, though: spreadsheet management can be a full-time occupation, even a profession. The two basic tools you'll find most useful are error checking, and model management formulas.

Checking for Errors

Unfortunately, this activity is often glossed over by many spreadsheet developers, even experienced ones. There are three different types of common errors:

- **logic errors**: a formula may be wrong, or an important variable omitted;
- **implementation errors**: a bad reference or a wrong function;
- **usage errors**: a wrong value may be entered, or a correct value in the wrong place (these types of errors usually happen during decision-making, analysis or operations).

As you can tell by now, some of these errors are specific to certain stages of the spreadsheet process: developing or conceptualizing the model, implementing the logic, or using the finished product.

All errors are hard to identify, but usage errors are especially so. If you're creating a model for other people to use, obviously you're not responsible for any errors they make. Still, you can play an important role by providing users with the tools to more easily spot usage errors.

Developers themselves are usually bad at finding their own mistakes: they've been involved with the model for so long that they may look straight at a wrong formula without noticing anything amiss. And it's important to catch any errors (existing or potential) as soon as possible, to prevent them from accumulating. Think of your spreadsheet errors as like compounding interest charges: the longer they exist, the costlier they are. You might call such a situation spreadsheet debt.

That's why this section offers a few techniques to help you identify the presence of errors. Once you know they exist, it's easier for you to find where they are. One useful strategy, if you've become too familiar with a model to spot any mistakes, is to have a colleague verify your spreadsheet.

Another strategy is to test whether the values of your calculated and output variables make sense in terms of your original input variables. How do you recognize an obviously wrong value? Here are a few warning signs to look out for.

No Change

When you change the value of an input data variable, is there a calculated variable that doesn't change? The absence of such a change—in a variable that, according to your Formula Diagram, has a direct or an indirect relationship with the changed variable—is a sure sign that there's an error in some formula path linking the two.

Wrong Direction of Change

The direction of change is not what you expected. If you increase the price and sales go up, for instance, you probably have a problem.

Wrong Magnitude of Change

Does a small change in an input or a data variable cause a big change in a calculated variable? If you change the price by 1% and sales go up by 1000%, you should investigate the formula(s). If there's a good explanation for such a big change, you need to know what it is.

Similarly, if you make a big change in an input variable, and this creates only a small change in a calculated variable, this too should be investigated. If you double the price and your profit barely increases, take a closer look at the variables and formulas linking price to profit.

Negative Values

A negative profit is not unusual for a business having a bad sales period. But watch out for times when your spreadsheet tries to tell you that you have negative sales, or a negative number of employees.

Extreme Results

To find any errors or inconsistencies in your model, try some extreme values for input variables and data variables. Do the output values make sense? If not, try to identify the range where they do. It's normal for a model to have ranges of values for its input and data variables.

Using Model Management Formulas

As a developer, a useful way for you to enhance a spreadsheet—one that makes it easier to use, and prevents users from inputting values that don't make sense—is to include model management formulas. There are three types of these:

- **input-validation** formulas
- **model validation** formulas
- **unit-changing** formulas.

This section explains each formula in detail.

Input Validation Formulas

To reduce the possibility of entering incorrect data into models, you can include some formulas to check the validity of certain input and data variables—both single-value and repeating variables. The examples below illustrate how to approach these two cases.

Validating Single-Value Input and Data Variables. If an input variable is a product code, for example, a validation formula in the cell next to it would show the product name or description. This warns you if you entered an incorrect product code.

Validating Repeating Input and Data Variables. There's no set correct value for this formula; you can judge what's correct for your situation. In the case of a distribution data variable, for example, the sum should be 100%. For an indicator data variable, the sum should show the number of times the event occurs.

Another option is to show the minimum and maximum of a set of values. Calculating the ratio of the one to the other can reveal, for instance, whether a digit is missing in an input value (which would change the order of magnitude of an otherwise normal ratio).

One possibility would be:

$$IF(SUM(Distribution) <> 1; \text{“Error”;” ”})$$

Another possibility is:

$$\textbf{\textit{Total Distribution = SUM(Distribution)}}$$

$$\textbf{\textit{IF(Total Distribution <> 1; “Error”;” ”)}}$$

This second approach has the advantage of providing more information about the nature of the error.

If users want to enter last year's monthly sales, for instance, they might also enter last year's total sales, and verify that the sum of all monthly sales adds up to the total. This redundant data entry is usually a good validation—as long as the validation value (total sales) is calculated independently of the other values.

Model Validation Formulas

These formulas prevent the model from being used if unreasonable or unrealistic conditions are present, and help users to validate the calculations. For example, to ensure that an account sheet is balanced, the simple formula is:

$$\textbf{\textit{Total Assets – Total Liabilities and Equity.}}$$

If the model is correct, the result should be 0. If that's not the case, it indicates that there's a spreadsheet error.

Unit-Changing Formulas

Input data may come from sources that are outside the control of users. They may also be in measurement units that don't match users' own model: temperatures in Fahrenheit rather than Celsius, for example, or distances in miles rather than kilometers.

As you use the model, if it's built with one set of units but data is supplied in another, you have two options when you refresh the values of the input variables.

- The spreadsheet instructs you to convert the values manually to the proper units.
- You enter the values as you obtain them, and use unit-changing formulas in the spreadsheet to convert them to the proper units.

The first method is error-prone and time-consuming. The second method is not only quicker, since it requires less manipulation, but it also leaves the original data intact and visible—

allowing you to validate the input if needed. However, it's not quite error-proof. For example, a source may change its units, thereby rendering the use of the unit-changing formula incorrect.

Should the Formula Diagram show the unit-changing formulas? No, it should not. Unit-changing formulas do not contribute to the model, and they are usually only needed in specific circumstances that could change over time.

Your model should use a single-unit system, to avoid user confusion and to facilitate future maintenance. It's your choice whether to use metric or imperial, but make sure you don't have some variables using one system, and the rest using another.

As you create the spreadsheet, name the cell that contains the changed value. As shown in Figure 12-1, *Cell B4* contains the formula to change the units of the source data recorded in *Cell C4* from Fahrenheit degrees to Celsius degrees. It also shows that the cell name **Average Temperature** refers to *Cell B4*.

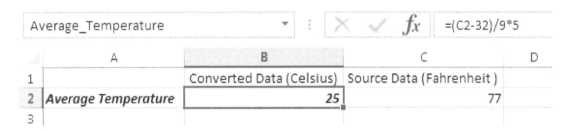

Figure 12-1 Using a Unit-Changing Formula

When it's time to refresh the data, you need only enter the new value you obtain from the data source into *Cell C4*. The model will work with the transformed value of *Cell B4*.

Protecting Worksheets

One final word on spreadsheet management: you may want to protect the formulas you develop, to prevent users from modifying them without proper controls and validations. All the specific cell contents are protected by default, but the worksheets themselves are not; and since the worksheet takes priority over the cells, they can in fact be modified. This means that you must determine which cells to protect or leave unprotected. The following strategies are best.

- **Data sheets**: All data variable cells should have their protection removed (these are easy to identify if you have formatted them with colour). However, the sheet itself should be protected.

- **Model sheets**: All these sheets, and all their cells, should be protected, since there is no reason for users to modify their content.

- **Interface sheet**: This should be left unprotected, since it's where users will analyze different scenarios.

Chapter 12 Overview

Here are the main points for you to remember from Chapter 12.

- Make these spreadsheet-management tasks a regular part of your development routine.

- While the conceptual model makes logical errors easier to spot, implementation errors are notoriously easy to make. As you're building the spreadsheet, keep your eye open for irregularities.

- Use checks in your model to try to catch errors. If possible, have someone else verify the spreadsheet.

- Protect certain aspects of the workbook, to prevent users from changing the formulas.

Part III Overview

The techniques and tips from Part III allow you to apply the SSMI methodology to various different scenarios. A key feature is the ability to maintain and manage the spreadsheet throughout its life cycle—an important task for both the model developer and the user.

- Here are the main points for you to remember from Part III.

- Reasons for modifying a spreadsheet may include a change in the problem structure, a user request for more functionality, or even the discovery of a mistake in the model logic. So it's important for you to be able to identify where the model needs improvement, and how to make the necessary changes.

- The Formula Diagram and the Formula List provide visual cues to help you understand the logic of the modification. These models allow you to immediately see what impact a change will have on the rest of your model, and what variables will be affected.

- Once you have adjusted the Formula Diagram and the Formula List, implementing the modification into the spreadsheet is usually straightforward.

- If you have a repeating sub-model or a temporal model, you only need to make the modifications in one column. Then you simply copy the new formulas over to the other columns to apply the change to all other instances.

- Modelling special cases is done by assuming a state of no exceptions. Some examples of ways to implement a special case into the model include using indicator variables, distribution data variables and allocation data variables. This ensures the transparency of your spreadsheet.

- Check for errors by noticing any irregularities in the results. You can also use model management formulas to ensure that your cells contain the correct type of data, and are making the correct calculations.

Conclusion

Spreadsheets have become such a popular tool mainly because of the flexibility of their programming language. Anyone can open up an Excel spreadsheet and enter formulas. However, the underlying art and science of modelling is much more difficult.

The ability to open a Word document and type some words is no guarantee of being able to write a book; and the same can be said about spreadsheet creation. Few people are able to model with little or no training—yet just as with creative writing, many people hold the misconception that they're quite good at it!

Spreadsheets are such an important source of error today, and the impact of this increasing error rate is now so great, that more and more attention is being paid to the risk and governance of spreadsheets. Especially in corporate settings, a lot of research and effort is being invested in developing audit processes and tools to verify spreadsheets.

This is a challenging task, because many spreadsheets are often hard—if not impossible—for anyone other than their creator to understand. (And after some time has passed, often even the creator may find it difficult to understand the original model.)

The only reliable way to understand what a spreadsheet does has traditionally been through a process of "reverse engineering": someone has to examine every formula to figure out what it's supposed to do. If errors are found, a fix for them must somehow be inserted into the existing formulas.

Some of this analysis even tries to produce an after-the-fact diagram representing the relationships between spreadsheet elements. By now, this idea should be familiar to you: it's the conceptual model—but created by working backward, rather than forward! This process is not only time-consuming and expensive, it's also highly inefficient.

That's the great benefit of the SSMI methodology: it allows spreadsheet creators to be proactive rather than reactive. If spreadsheets are properly structured and documented during their creation, they are less likely to contain errors. As well, they are much easier to comprehend, maintain and audit.

And no matter who initially designed and implemented the model, it can be handed off to another developer with a minimum of confusion. This not only makes life easier for both the creators and users of spreadsheets, whether internal or external; it also satisfies the governance requirements imposed by regulatory agencies.

I hope you've found this introduction to SSMI methodology useful and thought-provoking; and I hope that it'll enable you to make better future use of the powerful and flexible tool that is Excel. And while you solve your own spreadsheet issues, for your personal or work use, you may be encouraged by the thought that you're also part of a wider movement toward improving tomorrow's spreadsheets!

Feel free to share your thoughts and your new skills with others—and to recommend that they too learn the skills of Structured Spreadsheet Modelling and Implementation. For more information, visit our website at www.ssmi.international.

Appendix A Excel Toolbox

While Excel has hundreds of different functions, there are a few that you will use over and over. This section examines a number of handy Excel features and functions. While this list is by no means exhaustive, it describes some of the tools you may find most useful. The topics I'll cover here are:

- Naming Cells
- Using Names
- Formatting Cells
- Rounding
- Using Date Arithmetic
- Building Text Strings
- Table Lookup

Naming Cells

Naming single cells, or ranges, is the basis of efficient spreadsheet design, so it's important that you master this feature. There are many different ways to create names. The SSMI methodology is to always use the cell containing descriptive text that's situated to the left of (or above) the cells you want to name.

The first step in creating names is to select the cells you want to name, and the cells that contain the names. Then you follow these steps.

In Excel 2007 and later, select the *Formulas* tab, go to the *Define Names* group, and click the *Create From Selection* icon.

In Excel 2003 and earlier, select the *Insert menu*, choose *Name*, and then *Create*.

In all versions of Excel you can use the Alt keyboard codes: for Insert, Name and Create, just enter Alt+I, Alt+N and Alt+C in sequence.

The *Create from Selection* dialogue box gives you a choice of up to four options: *Top Row*, *Left Column*, *Bottom Row* and *Right Column*. The first two are the most commonly used. When you open the dialogue box, Excel examines your selected range and automatically presents one or two choices according to your data position. This means you may have to unselect non-appropriate options.

The three most common naming situations are outlined below.

Naming Single Cells.

Select both the names and the cells that contain the values. Figure A-1 illustrates naming the five cells from B3 to B7, using the names in A3 to A7.

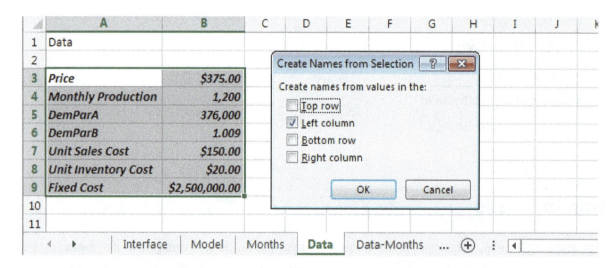

Figure A-1 Naming Single-Value Cells

Naming Rows or Columns.

Select the row or the column by clicking on the _row number_ or the _column letter_. To name a row, the name must be in _Column A_, referring to all cells starting from _Column B_. To name a column, the name must be in _Row 1_, referring to all cells starting from _Row 2_. As shown in Figure A-2, you can name _Row 7_ from _Column B_ to the end, **Monthly Demand**. This option allows you to name calculated variables and data variables that are part of a repeating sub-model.

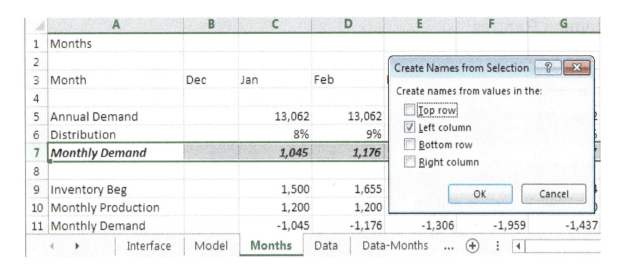

Figure A-2 Naming a Row

In a structured spreadsheet implementation, we name the rows containing a repeating variable definition. But we often receive data in the form of tables, where the first row of each column contains the data variable name as text and the other rows contain the data values. In this case, you make sure that the variable names are in *Row 1* of your worksheet and create all the variable names in one single naming operation, as illustrated in Figure A-3. Note our use of the plural form when we name table data and singular form when we name the variables using the table: it is then easier to discern the lookup variable used in the **LOOKUP** and **MATCH** functions from the lookup vectors.

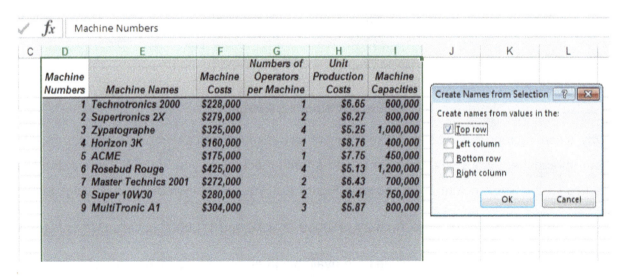

Figure A-3 Naming Columns

Naming Ranges.

Naming ranges lets you give a name to a rectangular shaped set of cells. It may be one of the most used ways of naming cells but I strongly discourage its use because it can also lead to errors later when your spreadsheet is modified. I will describe it because you will certainly encounter spreadsheets that use it and you need to know how it works so you can understand their formulas.

Select both the names and the set of values. Figure A-4 illustrates naming the *range D2:D10* **Machine Nos**, the *range E2:E10* **Machine Names**, the range *F2:F10* **Machine Prices**, the *range G2:G10* **Emps Per Machs**, the *range H2:H10* **Unit Mfg Costs** and the *range I2:I10* **Capacities**. This is usually done for data variables that have the form of a table, where you name the columns with the labels in the top row. You can then use the **LOOKUP**, **INDEX** and **MATCH** functions to use the proper value of from the table depending on some condition set in your model, like letting the user choose a **Machine Name** or **Machine Number**.

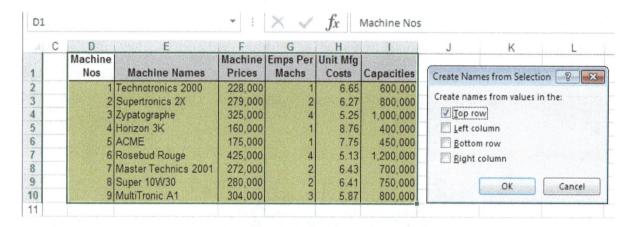

Figure A-4 Naming Ranges

Why is naming ranges a problem? Like I mentioned earlier, errors can crop up when you modify your spreadsheet. Let's say you want to add a tenth machine to your data. If you created the names for the whole columns, as shown in Figure A-3, you would then do the following step:

- add the values 10, Astro Tech 2V, 450000, 2, 4.76 and 1100000 in cells *D11* to *I11*.

That's it, you're done. The new values are available in all your spreadsheet formulas that use the 6 names.

Now, if you created range names as described in this section, you would then do the following step:

- add the values 10, Astro Tech 2V, 450000, 2, 4.76 and 1100000 in cells _D11_ to _I11_;
- select the _range D1:I11_;
- re-do the _Create Name from Selection_;
- click the _Yes button_ in the window asking you to confirm the name modification, six times.

And now, you're done. The new values are available in all your spreadsheet formulas that use the 6 names.

The way you create the names has no bearing on how you use them in **LOOKUP**, **INDEX** and **MATCH** functions. But there is so much potential for mistakes with range names:

- you can simply forget to re-do the name creation;
- you can make an error when you select the range:
- you can forget a column in your selection;
- you can even forget rows in your selection. (Yes, I've seen cases where the user selected fewer rows!)

You may think, now, that you would never make such mistakes. We all tend to be overconfident in our abilities. Remember that the probability of making mistakes increases with the number of operations you make to complete a task. Also, it may be someone else who will do the modification in the future, and they may not be knowledgeable about names.

For all those reasons, I don't recommend the use of range names. I haven't yet encountered a case where column names (or row names) couldn't be used.

Using Names

There are five ways to enter a name in a formula, as described below.

1) Type the whole name—a quick method when the name is short.

2) Start typing the name, and let Excel's auto-complete feature list the known functions and names that begin with those characters. As you type, the list shortens. At any time, you can use the arrows to scroll up or down the list (as shown in Figure A-5). When the name you want is highlighted, press the _Tab_ key, and Excel enters it in the formula.

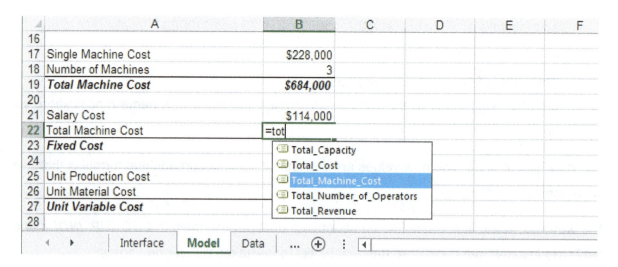

Figure A-5 Name Auto-Completion

3) Press the *F3* key to call up the *Paste Name* dialogue box. (All versions of Excel have this feature.) You can type a few letters to navigate quickly to the name you want, then use the arrow keys to finalize your choice. Clicking the *OK* button pastes your selected name into the formula. This process is shown in Figure A-6.

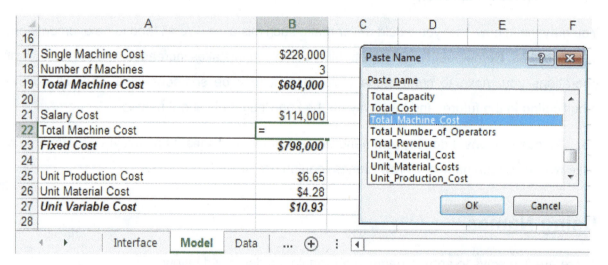

Figure A-6 The "Paste Name" Dialogue Box

4) Click the *Use in Formula* icon from the *Define Names* group in the *Formulas* tab, as shown in Figure A-7.

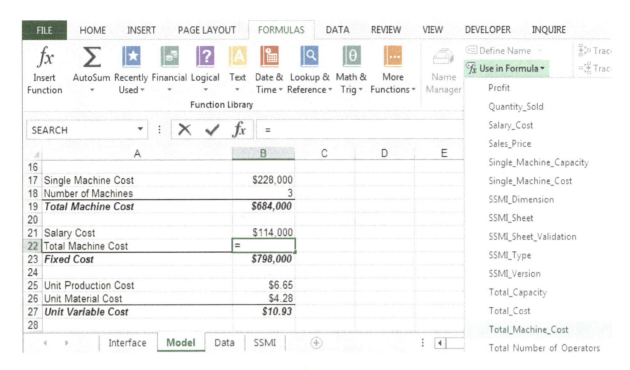

Figure A-7 The "Use in Formula" Icon

5) Navigate to the cell you want to use (if it's named, its name will automatically appear). A longer process, this is the least efficient way of entering single cell names; but it's useful if, for instance, you forget the cell's name. To use this method with range names, you need to select the whole range before Excel shows its name in the formula.

Formatting Cells

The design and format of the spreadsheet depends on the user's preference. For example, some companies may have colour palettes they use for their corporate documents, while others may have specific formatting conventions (decimal places, input identifiers, font sizes, etc.).

Because of this need for flexibility, the SSMI methodology does not insist on any one formatting style. That said, it's crucial for the understandability of your spreadsheet that your layout and design stays consistent; and that you indicate to users or viewers what conventions you use. Here are some suggestions to consider when formatting your cells.

Variable Definitions

To visually distinguish where variables are defined, it's a good idea to format them in **_bold-italic_**. In the case of calculated variables, it's also useful to set them off with a top border to help you differentiate the variables used in the formula (above the line) from the result (below the line).

Numbers

Formatting cells as you develop a model is a time-wasting activity. Whether for currency (price or cost), or for values such as quantities, distances, grades or percentages, you should limit yourself to only the most basic formatting. Use a thousand separator (comma or space, depending on your country's standard), and use an appropriate number of decimal places. You should be consistent in this: if you represent percentages with two decimals, do so throughout the model.

(It's best not to use any other formatting in the model sheets. You may do some formatting in the interface and data sheets, if you wish; but save it until the end, so it won't interfere with your implementation process.)

Input Variables

If you wish, you may identify Input cells with colour shading. It should be light enough so that the cell's content is easily visible, but dark enough so that the colour is visible in a black-and-white printout.

Conditional Format

This is a way to attract the user's attention to results when some predefined condition is met. For example, a high profit may be coloured green, and a loss red.

Rounding

The number of digits to the right of the decimal point is called the value's *precision*. Dollar values, for example, often have a precision of 2, though other currencies may be rounded to three figures.

Excel has two types of rounding: Value Rounding and Display Rounding.

- **Value Rounding** changes the precision of a number, and all subsequent calculations use the new precision.

- **Display Rounding** affects only the value shown on the screen or in a printout. All subsequent calculations use the full, unrounded, precision.

The latter type can cause some apparent incoherence, as illustrated in Figure A-8.

| F11 | | | | | f_x | =SUM(Rounded_Display_2) |

	A	B	C	D	E	F	G	H	I	J
1										
2	Seq No	Value	Rounded Value 1	Rounded Display 1	Rounded Value 2	Rounded Display 2				
3	1	0.125	0.1	0.1	0.13	0.13				
4	2	0.125	0.1	0.1	0.13	0.13				
5	3	0.125	0.1	0.1	0.13	0.13				
6	4	0.125	0.1	0.1	0.13	0.13				
7	5	0.125	0.1	0.1	0.13	0.13				
8	6	0.125	0.1	0.1	0.13	0.13				
9	7	0.125	0.1	0.1	0.13	0.13				
10	8	0.125	0.1	0.1	0.13	0.13				
11	Sum	1	0.8	1.0	1.04	1.00				

Figure A-8 Formula Rounding and Display Rounding

You must decide for yourself what degree of precision to use with different types of numbers. Quantities may be rounded to units, or to tens, hundreds or thousands of units. Once you decide on your format, use the **ROUND** function to make sure that your results are properly rounded.

(One Excel feature it's strongly advised **not** to use is _Precision As Displayed_. This option, which changes the number of displayed decimals in calculations, is often activated for purely cosmetic reasons—yet it can affect the precision of results, without users being aware of the fact.)

Even if you decide to round your results, you don't always need the **ROUND** function. Two situations when you can safely ignore it are:

- adding and subtracting numbers that already have the precision you wish,
- multiplying a number with the desired precision by any integer yields a result with the same precision.

Using Date Arithmetic

Excel treats dates as a special type of data. A date—which could be just a text value, such as July 15, 2015—might be a critical factor in some cases, such as calculating the expiry of a 90-day product warranty. This is where date arithmetic comes in handy. (And even if you don't need date arithmetic in your model, it's still a good idea to know how it works. This can simplify other aspects of developing spreadsheets.)

Date System

Computer programs use a date system based on an origin date, which associates a serial number with each date. The program counts the days sequentially, starting at 1 for the origin date. For example, if January 1, 2015 is your origin date, then January 15, 2015 would be serial number 15, February 1 of that same year would be serial number 31. December 31 2017 would be serial number 1096 (365, the number of days in 2015, 366, the number of days in 2016, which is a leap year, plus 365, the number of days in 2017), and so on.

Excel's default origin date—serial number 1—is January 1, 1900; but you don't need to know this, or the exact serial number of the dates you use. Excel automatically computes their serial number and stores it as the cell's value; then (rather than displaying a serial number in your spreadsheet) the program converts it to text.

Date Display

The way Excel displays a serial number is governed by the cell's format. When you enter a value that Excel interprets as a date, it calculates and memorizes a serial number. Then it automatically changes the cell's format to display the date in a format that resembles the input value. However, sometimes Excel's interpretation is not what you really want; you would rather have the date displayed right away, as opposed to having to calculate it yourself based on the serial number displayed. In such cases you can specify another number format.

Building Text Strings

Your spreadsheet might often contain labels identifying periods covered. For example, a sheet of sales forecasts for the next year may have a cell containing the text *Sales Forecast Oct-2015 to Sept-2016*. The next month, this would need to be changed to *Sales Forecast Nov-*

2015 to Oct-2016. This means you may often have to navigate through the different sheets and manually change the labels, which is a tedious and error-prone task. So is using Excel's Search and Replace feature, since this may inadvertently change some values that shouldn't be changed.

The solution to this problem is to create a special **Labels** sheet for labels and titles that change periodically. This sheet is not part of the model, but you should develop it using the same techniques: labels should be named and constructed with formulas, using calculated variables as needed. If you do this, minimal input is required. For example, changing many labels containing *Oct-2015 to Sept-2016* to *Nov-2015 to Oct-2016* can be done with just one input value.

Table Lookup

This feature is often used when data is presented in a tabular format, like a price list, a rebate form or a class roster. In such tables, some columns have unique values: no two lines have the same value. In a class roster, for example, student names may not necessarily be unique, but student IDs always are. In a price list, product names and descriptions are usually not unique, but product numbers are. The column used to identify each row of a table is the **key column**, and the lookup will be made there.

There are two kinds of lookup: exact lookup and approximate lookup.

- **Exact lookup** is pretty straightforward: you want to look up a student's name and program from the Student ID number, or a product's description, price and available quantity from its number. If the key column doesn't contain the lookup value, you need to know this fact so you can treat the situation with an appropriate formula.
- **Approximate lookup** can be considered as a form of range lookup: the key column indicates the beginning of each successive range.

As an example, let's consider a discount system where customers save more by buying a product in bulk. The discount offered is:

- 0% for quantities less than 5
- 4% for quantities of 5–9
- 6% for quantities of 10–24
- 8% for quantities of 25–49

- 10% for quantities of 50–99

- 15% for quantities of 100 and up.

As you can see in Figure A-9 the key column is named **From**. If the quantity bought is 15—even though there's no actual row with the key value of 15—you'll use the row identified by 10 to calculate the discount: 6%. (The **To** column is not really important, but most tables include it for ease of reading.)

	A	B	C	D
1	From	To	Discount	
2	1	4	0%	
3	5	9	4%	
4	10	24	6%	
5	25	49	8%	
6	50	99	10%	
7	100		15%	
8				

Figure A-9 Discount Table, Approximate Lookup

Using the LOOKUP Function

This is one of the many useful Excel functions that are not as well-known as they should be. It uses three arguments:

- the **lookup value**,

- the **key column** where Excel looks for that value,

- the **result column**, where the value in the corresponding row is displayed.

Figure A-10, uses the table shown above (Figure A-9) to illustrate the use of the **LOOKUP** function.

| Discount_Percentage | | ▾ | ⋮ | ✕ | ✓ | *fx* | =LOOKUP(B2,From,Discount) |

	A	B	C	D	E	F	G	H
1								
2	Quantity	15						
3	Discount Percentage	6%						

Figure A-10 LOOKUP Function

There are two rules for using **LOOKUP**:

- you must sort the **key column** in increasing order
- the **lookup value** must not be smaller than the **first key value**.

In some instances, the first restriction can be a problem. Consider the example of a product list. It's usually sorted alphabetically by product description because that's easier for people to use, as illustrated in Figure A-11.

	A	B	C
1	**Codes**	**Descriptions**	**Unit Prices**
2	2002	Business Card Holder Pages, Untabbed, Clear, 5/Pack	4.87
3	4181	Insertable Plastic Dividers, Multicolour, 5-Tab Set	1.18
4	7506	Insertable Plastic Dividers, Multicolour, 8-Tab Set	1.25
5	4706	Page-Size Sheet Protectors, Clear, 50/Pack	8.89
6	6949	Standard Clear Sheet Protectors	6.38
7	3448	White Self-Adhesive Reinforcements, 200/Pack	1.98
8	7766	White Self-Adhesive Reinforcements, 225/Pack	2.34
9	3085	Write-On Dividers, Multicolour, 5-Tab Set, 3/Pack	5.76

Figure A-11 Product List

Using a **LOOKUP** function using the product description would require a lot of typing for the user, as shown in Figure A-12 and Figure A-13.

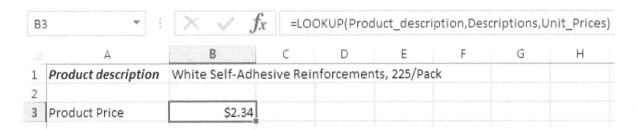

Figure A-12 LOOKUP by Product Description

In cases like this, it's much easier to ask the user to enter the product code instead of its description. But the **LOOKUP** function will not work properly, as shown in Figure A–12.

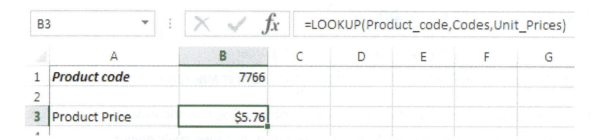

Figure A-13 LOOKUP by Product Code

Sorting the Product List by *Codes* is not a solution to this problem; there might be other formulas in the spreadsheet that depend on the list being sorted by the *Descriptions* and they, in turn, will stop working properly.

In this case, the combined use of the *MATCH* and *INDEX* functions allow you to keep the table sorted for the use by a human being at all times, while having a working formula in your model.

Using the MATCH Function

The *MATCH* function is similar to *LOOKUP*; but rather than returning for the value found in another column, it returns the position of the item in the key column. That position, stored in a named cell, is useful in conjunction with the *INDEX* function. The *MATCH* function requires three arguments:

- the *lookup value* used for the search;
- the *key column* in which to perform the search;
- a *match code* indicating the type of search to perform: 0 is used to indicate that you want an exact match.

Figure A-14 gives an example of the *MATCH* function.

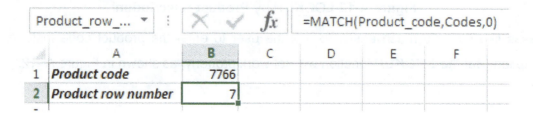

Figure A-14 MATCH Function

Using the INDEX Function

The **INDEX** function returns the value of a cell at a specified position. It uses two or more arguments:

- the range in which the value is located;
- the row number within that range;
- the column number within that range. This argument is optional: if you don't specify it, the first column will be used.

Figure A-16 shows the normal view and Figure A-16 the formula view of the two steps needed to use **MATCH** and **INDEX** together.

	A	B
1	Product code	7766
2	Product row number	7
3	Product Price	$2.34

Figure A-15 INDEX and MATCH

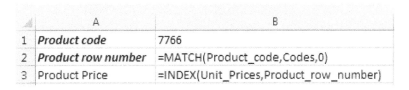

	A	B
1	Product code	7766
2	Product row number	=MATCH(Product_code,Codes,0)
3	Product Price	=INDEX(Unit_Prices,Product_row_number)

Figure A-16 INDEX and MATCH (Formula View)

Appendix B Glossary

Term	Definition
Aggregate function	A function that take a set of values and return a single value.
Application	A program that implements a system's business logic.
Backward approach	A modelling technique that starts with a variable and determines what other variables are needed to produce it.
Black box	A device, system or object that people use without actually knowing how it works.
Block structure	The structured way of implementing a definition formula, with the referenced variables above the separating line and the formula itself below.
Calculated variable	A variable computed by a formula that uses other variables.
Conceptual model	An information-systems technique that represents a problem graphically. The model employs the user's own vocabulary, and doesn't depend on the technology that will be used to implement it.
Corkscrew	A common name used to illustrate a time reference formula.
Data variable	A variable whose value is set as a constant, and does not change.
Data sheet	The worksheet where all the data variables, including the inputs, are defined. It's one of the three types of worksheets in the three-tier architecture.
Definition formula	A formula used to define a calculated variable.
Developer	A person who contributes to building a system.
Formula Diagram	The conceptual model of a spreadsheet, giving a visual view of the variables and their relationships.
Formula List	The logical model of a spreadsheet, listing all the variables used in the model with their names, types, and values/formulas.
Formula output	The result produced by a formula.

Term	Definition
Forward approach	A modelling technique that uses existing variables to determine what new variables can be created.
Handing off	The act of passing on a spreadsheet to someone else, either for their personal use or for further development.
Illusion of Productivity	The misconception users have that by opening a spreadsheet and starting to enter values, they are being productive.
Illusion of Simplicity	The idea that if there are no rules, a spreadsheet task is easy.
Implementation	The process of creating the physical model of a system, performed with the help of the conceptual and logical models.
Information systems	A set of tools—computer programs, databases and processes—that are needed to make an organization function efficiently.
Input	The spreadsheet data variables whose values are changed by the user.
Instance	A value specific to one case of a repeating entity.
Interface sheet	The worksheet where the values of the input variables are entered, and the values of the output variables are displayed.
IT specialist	The technologist who implements the physical model using the logical model.
Logical model	An intermediary between the conceptual and physical model. It provides an overview of the user's needs in terms that can be understood technically.
Maintenance	The operation of correcting and enhancing a system to satisfy changing needs.
Model sheet	The worksheet where calculated variables are defined, one of the types of worksheets in three-tier architecture.
Modelling	The creative process of conceptualizing a problem, often using a visual representation that shows an overview of all the variables and their relationships to one another.
Module	A self-contained portion of a program with specific inputs, and the instructions to manipulate them to produce the desired output.
Multiple-value variable	A variable that represents a set of values, with one value for each instance of its repeating entity.

Term	Definition
Name reference	A reference formula that refers to a variable by its defined name.
Output	The results the user wants to see.
Physical model	The implementation of the information system, which requires a technical vocabulary and knowledge specific to that system.
Range name	The name used to define either a single spreadsheet cell, or a set of cells.
Reference formula	A simple formula that refers to where a variable is originally defined.
Repeating entity	The subject of a repeating sub-model that is implemented with each of its instances.
Repeating sub-model	A portion of a model where each variable represents a set of values, one for each instance of a repeating entity.
Sign-changing reference formula	A way to represent a subtraction, this by including the negative sign directly in the reference formula. It visually indicates to the user when a value is subtracted.
Spreadsheet architecture	The layout of a spreadsheet; how information is organized and presented.
Spreadsheet life-cycle	The stages of a spreadsheet's life, from its development to testing, maintenance, and end of use.
System analyst	The intermediary between the user and the IT specialist, the analyst produces a conceptual model from information provided by the user, and translates it into a logical model that can be understood by the IT specialist.
Three-tier architecture	A software engineering technique that consists of separating three major tasks performed by systems; building them separately; and connecting them with the appropriate relationships.